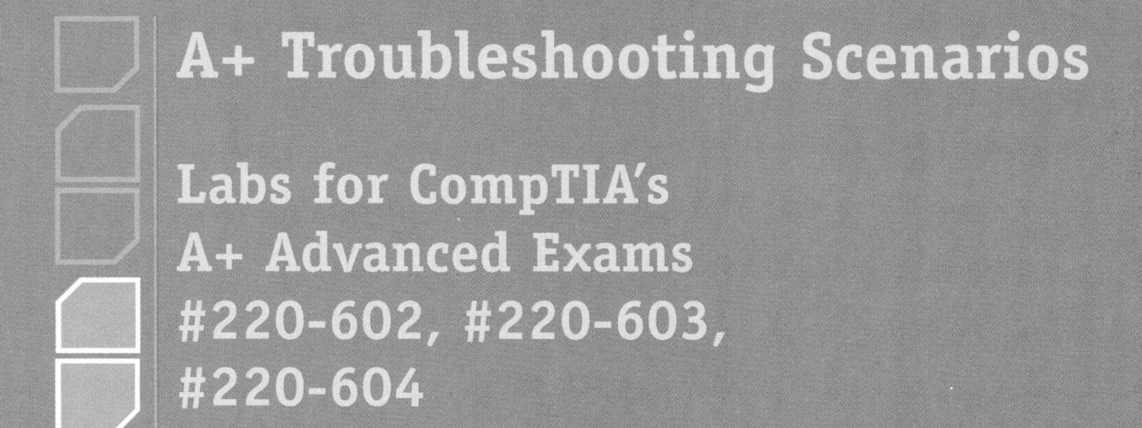

A+ Troubleshooting Scenarios

Labs for CompTIA's A+ Advanced Exams #220-602, #220-603, #220-604

Jean Andrews, Ph.D.

Australia • Canada • Mexico • Singapore • Spain • United Kingdom • United States

A+ Troubleshooting Scenarios is published by Thomson Course Technology.

Executive Editor:
Steve Helba

Managing Editor:
Larry Main

Acquisitions Editor:
Nick Lombardi

Senior Product Manager:
Michelle Ruelos Cannistraci

Developmental Editor:
Lisa Ruffolo

Marketing Manager:
Guy Baskaran

Print Buyer:
Julio Esperas

Content Project Manager:
Matthew Hutchinson

Technical Editor:
John Bosco, Green Pen QA

Copy Editor:
Kathy Orrino

Proofreader:
Andy Smith, Green Pen QA

Indexer:
Rich Carlson

Internal Design:
Betsy Young

Compositor:
Integra, Inc.

Printed in the United States of America
1 2 3 4 5 6 7 8 9 CK 10 09 08 07 06

For more information, contact
Thomson Course Technology, 25 Thomson Place,
Boston, Massachusetts, 02210.

Or find us on the World Wide Web at: www.course.com

ISBN-13 978-1-4283-2045-1

ISBN-10 1-4283-2045-8

Brief Contents

Table of Contents

CHAPTER 4

CHAPTER 5

CHAPTER 6

CHAPTER 7

CHAPTER 8

APPENDIX A

APPENDIX B

Introduction

A+ Troubleshooting Scenarios highlights the exam objectives for the three new A+ advanced certification exams from CompTIA: A+ 220-602, A+ 220-603, and A+ 220-604. Focusing on the knowledge and skills you need to pass these advanced exams, each chapter presents typical scenarios that confront PC repair professionals on the job. How should you respond when users report their computers are running more slowly than normal? Where do you start diagnosing problems with a dead laptop? What do you do to solve network connection failures? Complete the labs in this book to troubleshoot and solve these and other advanced computer problems.

You start each chapter by reviewing the objectives and content of particular advanced exam domains, and then engage in a lab designed to give you hands-on practice for meeting those objectives. You troubleshoot problems presented in a real-life scenario, performing tasks and answering questions that guide you to a solution. Finally, you secure your knowledge by responding to review questions and taking a practice exam. When you're finished, you'll have the skills to succeed on the job and on the A+ advanced certification exams.

Because the popularity of the CompTIA A+ certification credential is quickly growing among employers, becoming certified increases your ability to gain employment, improve your salary, and enhance your career. To find more information about A+ Upgrade Certification and its sponsoring organization, CompTIA, go to the CompTIA Web site at *www.comptia.org*.

FEATURES

To make the book function well for the individual reader as well as in the classroom, you'll find these features:

- **Summary of Domain Content:** Every chapter opens with a summary overview of the content in the CompTIA A+ advanced certification exams.
- **Objectives:** Each scenario lists learning objectives that set the stage for students to absorb the scenario's lessons.
- **Materials Required:** This feature outlines all the materials students need to complete the lab successfully.
- **Lab Preparation:** This feature alerts instructors and lab assistants to items to check or set up before the lab begins.
- **Scenario Background:** A brief discussion at the beginning of each scenario provides background information to help students understand the content.
- **Estimated Completion Time:** To help students plan their work, each lab estimates the total time required to complete the activities.
- **Scenario and Troubleshooting:** This section includes a scenario that describes a typical PC repair problem and provides questions and steps to troubleshoot the problem.
- **Figures:** Where appropriate, photographs of hardware and screenshots of software are provided to increase student mastery of the topic.

- **Review Questions:** Questions at the end of each scenario help students test their understanding of the content.
- **Practice Exams:** Each chapter concludes with questions similar to those presented on the CompTIA A+ advanced certification exam.

Notes

- **Notes:** Note icons highlight additional helpful information related to the subject being discussed.

Caution

- **Caution Icons:** These icons highlight critical safety information. Follow these instructions carefully to protect the PC and its data and also for your own safety.

INSTRUCTOR RESOURCES

Answers to all end-of-chapter material, including Review Questions and Practice Exams, are provided to instructors online at the textbook's Web site at *www.course.com/pcrepair*.

ORGANIZATION

Each chapter in the book addresses one of the eight domains measured on the advanced A+ exams. The table below lists these domains and the percentage weight they represent on the three advanced exams.

Chapter	Domain	Percentage of A+ 220-602	Percentage of A+ 220-603	Percentage of A+ 220-604
1	Personal Computer Components	18%	15%	45%
2	Laptop and Portable Devices	9%		20%
3	Operating Systems	20%	29%	
4	Printers and Scanners	14%	10%	20%
5	Networks	11%	11%	
6	Security	8%	15%	5%
7	Safety and Environmental Issues	5%		10%
8	Communication and Professionalism	15%	20%	
	Total	100%	100%	100%

LAB SETUP INSTRUCTIONS

LIST OF MATERIALS AND OPERATING SYSTEMS

Each lab begins with a list of required materials. All the equipment required for all the labs is listed here for your convenience:

- A computer designated for disassembly
- A PC toolkit with an antistatic ground strap and mat, screwdrivers, can of compressed air (or antistatic vacuum), contact cleaner, cotton swabs, isopropyl alcohol (not rubbing alcohol), sticky tape (or duct tape), soft cloth (or antistatic monitor wipes), and plastic cable ties
- An LCD monitor

- A computer running Windows XP with wireless capability
- A working notebook computer
- A notebook computer designated for disassembly and the notebook's technical reference manual that contains instructions for disassembly
- A projector (a monitor can be substituted)
- Windows XP setup CD or files on the setup CD available from another location
- Laser printer
- Scanner and scanner drivers
- A small network using a router that connects to the Internet using DSL or cable modem
- A wireless access point, such as a multipurpose router

Some labs might not have all of the above equipment available, but it is possible to improvise. For example, if you don't have a notebook available for each student to disassemble, the instructor can disassemble a single notebook as students watch and take notes. Also, if you don't have a laser printer available in your lab, you can take students to an office on campus where one is available and perform a demonstration using this office printer.

ACCESS TO THE INTERNET

Many of the labs require access to the Internet. For some of the labs, it is possible to download particular files from the Internet before lab begins and bring these files to lab on some sort of storage media. For labs that don't have Internet access, it is suggested that students perform these Internet lab activities as homework.

ACKNOWLEDGMENTS

When CompTIA made recent organizational changes to the 2006 A+ exams, we here at Course Technology and Delmar began to brainstorm ways to fully prepare the students for the advanced exams. These exams focus mostly on troubleshooting, so out of that concept came the idea for this book. Many thanks to Lisa Ruffolo, Matthew Hutchinson, Michelle Ruelos Cannistraci, Nick Lombardi, and Steve Helba for rousingly supporting this idea and helping to make it happen. The following reviewers all provided invaluable insights and showed a genuine interest in the book's success: Thank you to Arnold Abate, Hudson Valley Community College; Michael Avolese, Virginia College; C. Thomas Gilbert, Monroe Community College; Linda Glassburn, Cuyahoga Community College; Gus Chang, Heald College; and Paul Bartoszewicz, Florida Keys Community College. Thank you to Joy Dark who was here with me making this book happen. I'm very grateful.

This book is dedicated to the covenant of God with man on earth.

— Jean Andrews, Ph.D.

WANT TO WRITE THE AUTHOR?

If you'd like to give any feedback about the book or suggest what might be included in future books, please feel free to e-mail Jean Andrews at jean.andrews@buystory.com.

PHOTO CREDITS

All photographs were made by my daughter, Joy Dark.

CHAPTER 1

Personal Computer Components

Troubleshooting scenarios in this chapter:

- **Scenario 1.1:** Help Customers Make Upgrade Decisions to Improve Performance
- **Scenario 1.2:** Troubleshoot Video Problems
- **Scenario 1.3:** Troubleshoot a Hardware Problem

SUMMARY OF DOMAIN CONTENT

A+ 220-602
A+ 220-603
A+ 220-604

This section of the chapter contains a summary overview of the content in the CompTIA A+ 220-602, 220-603, and 220-604 combined objectives for Domain 1, *Personal Computer Components*. The high-level objectives for this domain are:

- Install, configure, optimize and upgrade personal computer components
- Identify tools, diagnostic procedures and troubleshooting techniques for personal computer components
- Perform preventive maintenance of personal computer components

Note

This summary of domain content assumes that you are already familiar with the content and only need a quick review. As you read, if you find a term or statement you don't understand, please refer to full-length textbooks such as *A+ Guide to Managing and Maintaining Your PC*.

INSTALL, CONFIGURE, OPTIMIZE AND UPGRADE PERSONAL COMPUTER COMPONENTS

Add, remove and configure personal computer components including selection and installation of appropriate components for example:

- ***Storage devices***
  - Storage devices include hard drives, optical drives, removable flash memory devices, and floppy drives. Most new PCs don't have a floppy drive.
  - Devices can be internal or external devices. Internal optical drives and hard drives can use a PATA connection to the motherboard or the newer and faster SATA connection. Internal high-density floppy drives use a 34-pin connector to the motherboard and hold 1.44 MB of data.
  - External devices can be attached using a USB port, 1394 (FireWire) port, Fibre Channel, SCSI, and eSATA. External SCSI and Fibre Channel connections are seldom used for personal computer systems. eSATA is faster than USB or FireWire, but more expensive. eSATA is rated at 2400 Mbs; FireWire 800 is rated at 800 Mbs; FireWire 400 is rated at 400 Mbs; USB 1.1 is rated at 12 Mbs; and USB 2.0 is rated at 480 Mbs.
- ***Drive preparation (220-604 only)***
  Current internal PATA drives are installed using an 80-conductor cable that has 40 pins and 80 wires. The maximum length of the cable is 18 inches. The cable can accommodate two drives, and the motherboard has two connectors, allowing a total of four PATA drives in a system.
- ***Jumper configuration (220-604 only)***
  Jumpers are set on each PATA drive to determine if the drive will be the master drive on the PATA cable or the slave drive. If only one drive is using the cable, set the jumpers to the Single selection. If no Single selection is available, set the jumpers to the Master selection. When using a cable select cable, ignore the jumpers on the drive—the position of the drive on the cable (end or middle) determines the master or slave setting.
- ***Storage device power and cabling (220-604 only)***
  One power cable connects a drive to the power supply using a 4-pin Molex connector. Floppy drives use a smaller Berg connector. SATA drives sometimes have two power

connectors on the drive: a Molex connector and a newer SATA power connector. Use only one connector with a single power cable to power the drive.

- ***Motherboards***
  Form factors for motherboards include ATX, Enhanced ATX, MiniATX, MicroATX, FlexATX, BTX, MicroBTX, NanoBTX, PicoBTX, NLX, and the older and outdated AT and Baby AT form factors. The chipset on the motherboard and the type of processor socket or slot determine the processor the board can support. The type and number of expansion slots on the board determine the expansion cards the board can support, and the memory slots and chipset determine the memory the board supports.
- ***Selection and installation of appropriate motherboard (220-604 only)***
  Match the form factor of the motherboard to that of the case and power supply. You must also match the processor, memory modules, and expansion cards to what the board is designed to support. Install the motherboard using an ESD bracelet and be sure to use spacers between the board and the case to protect circuits on the bottom of the board from shorting on the case.
- ***BIOS setup and configuration (220-604 only)***
  Enter BIOS setup by pressing a certain key during the boot. While in BIOS setup, you can configure settings such as system date and time, floppy drive type, hard drive type, hard drive settings, boot features, power-on password, supervisor password, parallel port mode, power management features, boot sequence, processor operating speed (for overclocking and throttling), and system bus speed. When you exit BIOS setup, the system reboots and applies your changes.
- ***Power supplies***
  A power supply converts AC to DC and changes the ratio of current to voltage to increase current and decrease voltage. Incoming voltage can be 110 V or 220 V AC, and output voltage can be 3.3, 5, and 12 Volt DC, depending on the form factor of the power supply. Form factors include ATX, ATX12V, MicroATX, BTX, LPX, NLX, and the older AT form factor. The power pinouts for the ATX and BTX power supplies are the same, and in many situations, can be interchanged. When selecting a power supply, consider the form factor, the number and type of power cables, venting, and the overall wattage rating of the power supply. Match the power supply form factor to the case and motherboard, and match the power supply wattage to the demands of the system.
- ***Processors/CPUs***
  Most motherboards can support two or three different types of processors that use the same type processor slot or socket. A board is designed to support either Intel or AMD processors. Read the motherboard documentation to find out which processors a board can support, and then select a matching brand, socket, model, and processor speed. Some high-end motherboards have two processor sockets so they can support dual processors.
- ***Selection and installation of appropriate CPU (220-604 only)***
  Match a processor to the motherboard. The motherboard documentation tells you the exact brands, models, and speeds of processors the board can support. For best performance, use the fastest processor the board will support and also consider other processor features such as the amount of onboard cache and whether it allows dual core.
- ***Memory***
  The type and speed of memory modules must match what the motherboard supports. Current memory module types include 240-pin DDR2 DIMMs, 184-pin DDR DIMMs, 168-pin SDR DIMMs, and 184-pin RIMMs.
- ***Selection and installation of appropriate memory (220-604 only)***
  Select the type of memory module and the speed of the module to match what the motherboard can support. When upgrading memory, use the same speed modules as

> **Note**
>
> For a complete listing of CompTIA A+ acronyms, see Appendix A.

those already installed. Install the number of modules in specific memory slots according to the motherboard documentation. Also, the size of each module installed must match the documentation. Other factors to consider are buffered or registered DIMMs, dual channeling, CAS latency, error-checking ability (ECC), and tin or gold leads.

- *Display devices*
  Types of display devices include CRT and LCD monitors and projectors. Select a high-end monitor to install in a system that has a high-end video card, and select a low-end monitor to match a low-end video card. Video cards might have VGA, S-Video, DVI, and Composite video ports. A video card might use an AGP, PCI, or PCI Express x16 slot. For extremely high-end video, two SLI video cards designed by NVIDIA can be installed in two PCI Express x16 slots with a bridging mechanism linking the two cards together. The motherboard must support this feature.
- *Input devices (e.g., basic, specialty and multimedia)*
  Basic input devices include a keyboard and mouse, which use a 6-pin mini-DIN or USB connector. Examples of specialty devices are touch screens, trackballs, touch pads, barcode readers, microphones, and fingerprint readers. A fingerprint reader is an example of a biometric device.
- *Adapter cards*
  An adapter card is installed in a slot on the motherboard, which can be a PCI (32-or 64-bit data path), PCI-X, PCI Express (x1, x4, x8, or x16), or AGP (1x, 2x, 4x, or 8x). AGP is used exclusively for video. For some PCI and AGP slots, be sure to match the slot voltage to the voltage required by the card. When selecting an adapter card, consider the type of ports provided on the back of the card and other card features.
- ***Installation of adapter cards including hardware and software/drivers (220-604 only)***
  Drivers are installed before or after the card is installed; follow manufacturer directions. Match drivers to the card and to the installed OS. After the drivers and card are installed, you can update the drivers using Device Manager.
- ***Configuration and optimization of adapter cards including adjusting hardware settings and obtaining network card connection (220-604 only)***
  Use Device Manager to verify the OS recognizes the card and it is installed in the OS with no errors. Also use Device Manager to enable and disable a device and update its drivers. Use lights on the back of a NIC to verify connectivity. You can use the Ping command to further verify connectivity to the network.
- *Cooling systems*
  - You can use BIOS setup to find out the inside temperature of the case and the processor. Computers use properly placed fans and heat sinks inside the case to keep the motherboard and processor cool. For additional cooling of overclocked systems, you can use refrigeration, peltiers, and water coolers.
  - To adjust for overheating, remove dust from inside the case and improve airflow by removing obstructions to air vents outside the case, installing faceplates on all bays and expansion card slots, and tying back cables that might obstruct airflow. Consider that the processor cooler is not properly installed and that additional case fans are needed.
  - All cooling methods except peltiers rely on airflow to cool. A peltier uses electricity to reduce air temperature and can be installed to replace other coolers when a computer is in a hot environment such as a hot warehouse.

Add, remove and configure systems (220-604 only)

- BIOS is installed on firmware on the motherboard, and the BIOS configuration utility is accessed by pressing a key at startup. BIOS can be updated with downloads from the manufacturer Web site. The configuration utility is called CMOS setup and includes settings for floppy drives, hard drives, motherboard ports and other onboard devices, power-on passwords, CPU, date, time, power management, and logging events at startup.
- When replacing the CPU or memory, the new device must match what the motherboard supports. Match a new motherboard to the case and power supply. Consider the new board might not support the current processor or memory.
- When CMOS settings are lost, chances are the CMOS battery needs replacing.

IDENTIFY TOOLS, DIAGNOSTIC PROCEDURES AND TROUBLESHOOTING TECHNIQUES FOR PERSONAL COMPUTER COMPONENTS

Identify and apply basic diagnostic procedures and troubleshooting techniques

When faced with a PC problem, follow these general guidelines:

1. Interview the user to determine what has recently happened, identify the problem and its symptoms, and find out how to reproduce the problem.
2. If possible, back up important data on the hard drive that has not been backed up.
3. Decide if the problem is hardware or software related.
4. Check simple things first and then apply the least-obstructive fixes.
5. Verify the fix to the satisfaction of you and the user.
6. Document the symptoms, problems, fixes, and outcomes.

- *Isolate and identify the problem using visual and audible inspection of components and minimum configuration*
  Carefully observe as you reproduce the problem. You can eliminate many sources to the problem by reducing the hardware to a minimum configuration or simplifying the startup process.

Recognize and isolate issues with peripherals, multimedia, specialty input devices, internal and external storage and CPUs (220–602 and 220–603 only)

One common method is to trade a good part for a suspected-bad part or to install a suspected-bad part into a working system.

Identify the steps used to troubleshoot components (e.g., check proper seating, installation, appropriate component, settings and current driver) for example:

- *Power supply*
  Check all power connections. Reduce the system to essentials. Trade good for suspected bad.
- *Processor/CPUs and motherboards*
  Suspect overheating when the system hangs after running for a while. Beep codes at startup or a dead system might mean a faulty motherboard or processor.

A motherboard communicates errors at startup as text messages on screen, beep codes, or voice messages.

- *Memory*
  Intermittent errors might be caused by faulty memory modules. At startup, BIOS might be configured to display a count of available RAM on screen and should match the amount of RAM installed. Use the Windows System Information window (Msinfo32.exe) to verify installed RAM.
- *Adapter cards*
  Use Device Manager and Event Viewer to check for errors with adapter cards. Some errors are detected at startup and reported on screen before Windows loads.
- *Display and input devices (202-602 only)*
  Use controls on the front of the monitor to check monitor settings and also verify the monitor is plugged in and turned on. Display settings in Windows can cause errors. Try reinstalling device drivers. Check cable connections and exchange a known-good device for a suspected-bad mouse, keyboard, or monitor.

Recognize names, purposes, characteristics and appropriate application of tools for example:

- *Multimeter*
  Used to verify a fuse is good, check cable pinouts, and check older power supply voltage output.
- *Anti-static pad and wrist strap*
  Used to protect a system against ESD while you are working on it.
- *Specialty hardware/tools*
  Many product manufacturers supply special tools to maintain their products. For example, a printer manufacturer might provide a brush for cleaning inside the printer. In these situations, use only those tools provided or recommended by the manufacturer.
- *Loop back plugs*
  Used to verify a port is good.
- *Cleaning products (e.g., vacuum, cleaning pads)*
  Keep dust out of the inside of a computer case using an anti-static vacuum cleaner or cans of compressed air. Cleaning pads can be used on monitor screens. Don't use a regular vacuum cleaner inside a computer case.
- *Test related components and evaluate results (220-603 only)*
  Know how to test each hardware component you support. For example, for a printer, know how to print a test page.
- *Document activities and outcomes (220-603 only)*
  Most companies expect a technician to document each service call or problem-solving project.

Apply steps in troubleshooting techniques to identify problems (e.g., physical environment, functionality and software/driver settings) with components including display, input devices and adapter cards (220-603 only)

Decide if a problem is software or hardware related. Given a list of solutions to a problem, always choose the one that makes as few changes as possible to a system.

PERFORM PREVENTIVE MAINTENANCE OF PERSONAL COMPUTER COMPONENTS

Identify and apply common preventive maintenance techniques for personal computer components, for example:

- *Display devices (e.g., cleaning, ventilation)*
  Maintain enough space around a monitor for proper ventilation. Clean the monitor screen with cleaning pads or a dry cloth.
- *Power devices (e.g., appropriate source such as power strip, surge protector, ventilation and cooling)*
  Not all power strips include a surge protector. A surge protector guards against voltage spikes and surges but not against noise, brownouts, or blackouts (power outages). A UPS protects against brownouts, blackouts, spikes, and surges. For best protections, use a UL (Underwriters Laboratories) rated UPS. To prevent overheating, power devices should not be operated over extended time at maximum performance.
- *Input devices (e.g., covers)*
  Use plastic covers on keyboards in dusty environments.
- *Storage devices (e.g., software tools such as Disk Defragmenter and cleaning of optics and tape heads)*
  Clean optical discs only with cleaning solutions specifically designed for optical discs. Tape heads can be cleaned with a cleaning tape. Hard drives need regular maintenance including using Defrag, deleting temporary files, and updating Windows, device drivers, and applications. Keep current backups of the system state and important data.
- *Check Disk (220-603 only)*
  Chkdsk is used to repair hard drive errors and is available from the command prompt and the Disk Properties window. Use Chkdsk to repair errors and use Defrag to improve performance.
- *Thermally sensitive devices such as motherboards, CPUs, adapter cards, memory (e.g., cleaning, air flow)*
  To keep temperatures inside the computer case low, remove dust inside the case and make sure the case vents are unobstructed.
- *Air flow (e.g., slot covers, cable routing) (220-604 only)*
  To improve airflow inside a case, keep slot covers in place and cables tied out of the way of airflow. Remove obstructions from around the case that might block air vents.
- *Cleaning (e.g., optics, tape heads) (220-603 only)*
  Know how to clean tape heads and optical discs.
- *Adapter cards (e.g., driver/firmware updates) (220-604 only)*
  Use Device Manager to update device drivers. Follow manufacturer directions to update firmware on adapter cards. Updates can be downloaded from manufacturer Web sites.

SCENARIO 1.1: HELP CUSTOMERS MAKE UPGRADE DECISIONS TO IMPROVE PERFORMANCE

OBJECTIVES

The goal of this lab is to help you get comfortable with examining a system and making decisions about possible upgrades that might improve the system's performance. After completing this lab, you will be able to:

- Benchmark system performance and identify weaknesses that can be improved by upgrading certain hardware.
- Identify the motherboard, the processor, memory modules, and the hard drive installed in a system.
- Select a processor, memory modules, and hard drive suitable for upgrading the system.

MATERIALS REQUIRED

This lab requires the following:

- A computer designated for disassembly
- A PC toolkit with an anti-static ground strap and mat
- Access to the Internet using this or another computer

LAB PREPARATION

Before the lab begins, the instructor or lab assistant needs to do the following:

- Verify that a computer designated for disassembly is working and available to each student or workgroup.
- Verify Internet access is available or provide another access to the downloaded file for SiSoftware Sandra (*www.sisoftware.co.uk*).

SCENARIO BACKGROUND

Slow performance can be caused by software or by an OS that is not optimized or a hard drive that needs cleaning up. In these situations, a support technician needs to know how to optimize the hard drive, the OS, and other installed software. Adding more RAM, installing a second hard drive, or upgrading the processor can sometimes greatly improve a system's performance. A support technician needs to know how to make good decisions about hardware upgrades that might improve performance. In this lab, you will examine a system and make hardware upgrade decisions.

ESTIMATED COMPLETION TIME: 1.5 hours

SCENARIO

Mike works as an accountant for a local corporation and telecommutes about two days a week. He uses his two-year-old desktop computer for gaming, surfing the Web, and telecommuting. His daughter also likes to play her games when the computer is free. He says that when he first bought the PC, it ran great, but now the computer is slow to start up, downloading files from the Internet takes too long, and generally, he thinks the computer is just slower than it used to be. He is asking you to help him decide what upgrades might help.

Many times users think that upgrading hardware is the solution to a slow system, but before spending money on hardware, the first thing to do is to clean up Windows, applications, and the hard drive to make sure the problem is not software related. If the system was fast when it was new and is now slow, logically, the problem is not caused by hardware, but by how the system has been used, installed applications, available space on the hard drive, Windows errors, viruses, adware, and other software-related factors. In Chapter 3, you will learn how to clean up a sluggish Windows system. In this lab, you can assume that the software is not the problem and turn your attention to possible hardware upgrades to speed up a computer.

Over time, users install new applications, which might add tasks to the Windows startup process. These applications and their data use up hard drive space, and users can get in the habit of running multiple applications at the same time. All these factors can be overcome by upgrading hardware to accommodate the system's heavier workload.

TROUBLESHOOTING

Follow the procedure outlined in the following steps to time startup and examine a system for startup problems.

1. Power down the computer and turn it on. Using a watch with a second hand, note how many minutes are needed for the system to start. Startup is completed after you have logged onto Windows XP and the hourglass has disappeared. How long does startup take?

   ____

2. Describe any problems you observed during startup (for example, error messages or warnings).

   ____

   ____

Benchmarking software can be useful when searching for performance bottlenecks. Using SiSoftware Sandra (*www.sisoftware.co.uk*) or other benchmarking software such as PassMark Software (*www.passmark.com*), run a test to measure overall performance of the system and compare it to other systems for possible performance weaknesses. Follow these steps to use SiSoftware Sandra:

1. Open your browser and go to *www.sisoftware.co.uk*. Follow the links on this Web site to download the free version of Sandra. Double-click the compressed file saved on your computer to uncompress it. Double-click the .exe file to run the setup program.
2. When you finish the installation, Sandra will start. For Windows XP, you should see a screen similar to the one in Figure 1-1.
3. On the Tools tab, use the Performance Index icon to generate a performance index report of your computer.
4. Print the results of running the software. Based on these results, which areas are strongest and which areas are weakest on your system?

   ____

   ____

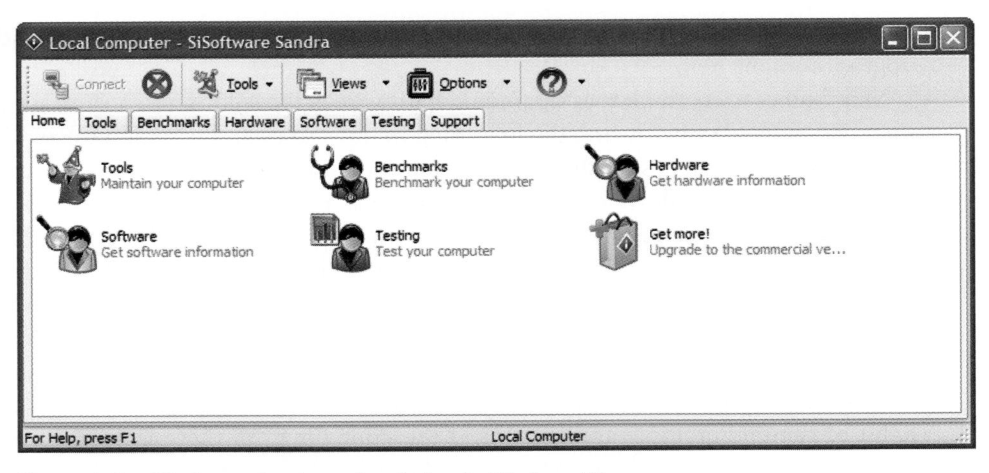

Figure 1-1 SiSoftware Sandra main window in Windows XP

In Table 1-1, list the information gathered about your system hardware. Useful sources of information include Device Manager, System Information, Control Panel, and the Properties dialog boxes for drives and devices.

Device	Description
Motherboard	**Brand:** ______
	Model: ______
	Chipset: ______
Processor	**Brand:** ______
	Model: ______
	Speed: ______
	Internal cache: ______
Memory	**Total installed RAM:** ______
	Type and size modules: ______
	Number of used memory slots: ______
	Number of empty memory slots: ______
	Amount of RAM this board supports: ______
Hard drive	**Brand:** ______
	Model: ______
	Speed (rpm): ______
	Size: ______
	Free space: ______
	Percentage of free space: ______

Table 1-1 Current system hardware

Answer the following questions:

- How did you determine the motherboard information?

  ____

  ____

- How did you determine the processor information?

  ____

  ____

- How did you determine the memory information?

  ____

  ____

  ____

- How did you determine the hard drive information?

  ____

  ____

  ____

Note

If the motherboard supports dual channeling, to use this feature you must use matching pairs of DIMMs in order to take advantage of the performance increase offered by dual channeling.

Now that you have gathered information about the system and its performance, you are ready to investigate the cost of upgrading hardware to improve performance. (Remember that for this lab, you are assuming that Windows, applications, and data are not a problem.) Do the following:

1. Does the motherboard allow a processor upgrade? If so, what processor can be installed? List the details of that processor and print a Web page showing the processor and its price.

   ____

2. What is the maximum amount of RAM this motherboard supports?

   ____

3. What memory modules must be purchased to upgrade RAM to a total of 2 GB or the maximum allowed RAM if that maximum is less than 2 GB? Print Web pages to show the cost of these memory modules.

   ____

4. Complete Table 1-2 to support your answer to Question 3.

Memory slot	Currently filled (Yes or No)	Description	Amount of RAM
1.			
2.			
3.			
4.			
5.			
6.			
		Total RAM currently installed: **Total RAM after upgrade:**	

Table 1-2 Planning a memory upgrade

Note

When selecting a new hard drive to improve performance in an existing system, try to choose a drive that is faster and larger than the original drive but can still be supported by the current motherboard. Consider the drive capacity (in GBs), interface (SCSI, SATA, or PATA), rotational speed (5400, 7200, or 10,000 RPM), buffer or cache (2 MB to 8 MB), and access time (lower milliseconds is better than higher milliseconds).

5. If Mike wants to add an extra 40 GB of hard drive space to the system, would you recommend installing a replacement hard drive or a second hard drive? Why?

____

____

6. What new hard drive would you recommend for a replacement drive? Print a Web page showing the price of the drive.

____

7. What new hard drive would you recommend as a second hard drive? Print a Web page showing the price of the drive.

____

8. If Mike decides he wants to spend no more than $400 total to upgrade the processor, memory, and/or the hard drive, what upgrades (if any) would you recommend and why?

____

____

REVIEW QUESTIONS

1. What is the transmission speed of USB 1.1? USB 2.0? 1394a? FireWire 800?

____

2. When improving startup performance, how can the Defrag command help you?

____

3. Describe the importance of the motherboard documentation in completing this lab.

____

4. For most systems, which hardware component can be upgraded to best improve performance?

____

5. When upgrading the processor, list three factors you need to consider when selecting a new processor.

____

6. When upgrading memory, explain how you can make sure dual channeling is enabled to make sure you have optimized memory performance.

____

7. How much free hard drive space is required so that Windows can completely defragment the hard drive?

____

SCENARIO 1.2: TROUBLESHOOT VIDEO PROBLEMS

OBJECTIVES

The goal of this lab is to help you learn to troubleshoot video problems. After completing this lab, you will be able to:

- Solve problems with the video subsystem.
- Investigate and update video card drivers.

MATERIALS REQUIRED

This lab requires the following:

- A working computer with Internet access
- An LCD monitor

LAB PREPARATION

Before the lab begins, the instructor or lab assistant needs to do the following:

- Verify the computer for each student or workgroup is working and has Internet access, and an LCD monitor is available.

SCENARIO BACKGROUND

The video subsystem includes the video card, video cable, and monitor. When solving problems with video, always check the simple things first. Monitor settings might be wrong or the video cable might be loose. Check these things before opening the case to check the video card.

Some applications, especially games and graphics programs, rely heavily on video. If an application is giving problems, one thing you can do is make sure the video card is using the latest drivers available for it. Also, if video is showing incorrect colors, streaks, or lines or is not working at all, you can try updating the video drivers. In this lab, you will find out what video drivers you are using and update them if an update is available.

ESTIMATED COMPLETION TIME: 1 hour

SCENARIO

You are the PC technical support person for a small accounting firm, and spend about one day a week at the firm addressing any technical problems that arise with computers, printers, scanners, fax machines, copiers, the network, and Internet access. One morning when you arrive at the firm, Larry, the owner, meets you at the door. He installed a really cool game (see Figure 1-2) on his desktop over the weekend, but notices that the game jumps and halts as he plays it. You know that gaming is generally not allowed on computers in the firm, but, oh, well, this is the boss, so you get down to business in solving his problem. The first thing you suspect is the video drivers. Sometimes the latest video driver is sufficient to solve a problem with a poorly responding game.

Figure 1-2 Using the latest video card drivers can often improve game performance

TROUBLESHOOTING

A PC support technician needs to know more than one way to do something. Complete the following to show two methods of viewing video driver files.

1. List the steps to view the details about video driver files.

____

____

2. How many video driver files are listed?

3. List the path and filename of three video driver files.

4. List the steps of a second method to view the list of video driver files.

5. List the path and filename of three more of the video driver files.

6. What is the name of your video card as shown in the Driver File Details window?

7. Identify the video card manufacturer and the URL of the manufacturer's Web site.

8. Search the Web site of the video card manufacturer for the latest drivers for this video card and download the drivers to a folder on your hard drive.
   - What is the path and filename of the downloaded file?
   - What is the version number of the video drivers?

9. Check the Web site for any special instructions for updating the drivers. For example, one site says to stop all antivirus software and uninstall the current driver using the Add or Remove Programs applet in Control Panel. What special instructions apply to your video card?

10. Follow the instructions to update the video drivers. List the steps you used here:

11. After the new video drivers were installed, what Display Properties settings did you have to reset?

12. Compare the filenames of the video drivers that you just installed to the older drivers previously installed. What differences do you see? How might this information be useful when troubleshooting video problems?

13. You might later decide to roll back the drivers. List the steps to do this.

On another day at the accounting firm, Jason, one of the staff accountants, asks for help with his monitor. He complains that his new LCD monitor is making it difficult for him to read large spreadsheets. He's tried adjusting the monitor settings, but still can't find the right combination of settings. Using an LCD monitor in your lab, answer the following questions:

1. Using hardware settings on the monitor, describe how to adjust the monitor brightness.

2. Using hardware settings on the monitor, describe how to adjust the monitor contrast.

3. Using hardware settings on the monitor, describe how to adjust the monitor color.

4. List the steps in Windows to smooth the edges of screen fonts to make the text sharper on screen.

5. List the screen resolutions the video drivers for this monitor support.

6. Can you adjust the screen settings so that text appears larger on the screen? If so, how?

____

____

____

While helping Jason, you notice his old CRT monitor sitting on the floor beside his desk collecting dust. You check the back of Jason's computer and find a video card with two ports, one a digital DVI port and the other a 15-pin analog port. The LCD monitor is connected to the 15-pin analog port using an analog video cable. The old CRT monitor also has an analog cable. List the steps and parts you would need to hook up the old monitor for a dual monitor system to help give Jason a little more Windows desktop space:

____

____

____

____

REVIEW QUESTIONS

1. Which expansion slot is faster, AGP 8x or PCI Express x16?

   ____

2. Before updating video drivers, you are asked to uninstall the current video drivers and restart the system. Why does the Found New Hardware Wizard launch when you restart the system?

   ____

3. What is one way to install the video drivers downloaded from the Internet?

   ____

4. List three situations where you might find it useful to update the video drivers.

   ____

5. Which tab of the Windows XP Display Properties window do you use to find the filenames of the video driver files?

   ____

6. What button on the tab in Question 5 do you use to access the video driver filenames?

   ____

SCENARIO 1.3: TROUBLESHOOT A HARDWARE PROBLEM

OBJECTIVES

The goal of this lab is to help you learn how to solve hardware-related PC problems. After completing this lab, you will be able to:

- Troubleshoot boot problems caused by hardware.

MATERIALS REQUIRED

This lab requires the following:

- A Windows XP computer designated for this lab
- Internet access

LAB PREPARATION

Before the lab begins, the instructor or lab assistant needs to do the following:

- Make available a Windows XP computer and verify that Internet access is available.

SCENARIO BACKGROUND

When a PC does not boot or boots with errors, the problem might be software or hardware related. After you have observed the problem, the next step is to make your best educated guess: Is the problem caused by hardware or software? Then begin troubleshooting from there. Sometimes as you work, you can accidentally create a new problem, so you need to always be aware that the problem might have more than one source. This lab takes you through some real-life troubleshooting situations to help build your troubleshooting skills.

ESTIMATED COMPLETION TIME: 1 hour

SCENARIO

John, a PC support technician, is in the habit of leaving his computer turned on when he leaves the office in the evening. Each morning, pressing a key returns the computer to activity from standby mode and he's good to go. However, one morning he sits down at his desk to discover a window with this information on screen:

```
P4P800 Asus Motherboard
Press DEL to run Setup
```

He recognizes the system is stuck at the very beginning of a restart, and the information on the screen is from startup BIOS. Follow along as John troubleshoots the problem.

1. He presses the Delete key and nothing happens. He tries other keys, but still no action. He tries pressing the power button on the front of the computer case, but that doesn't work either.

2. John unplugs the power cord to the system, plugs it back in, and presses the power button. The system powers up and hangs with the text shown in Figure 1-3 on screen.

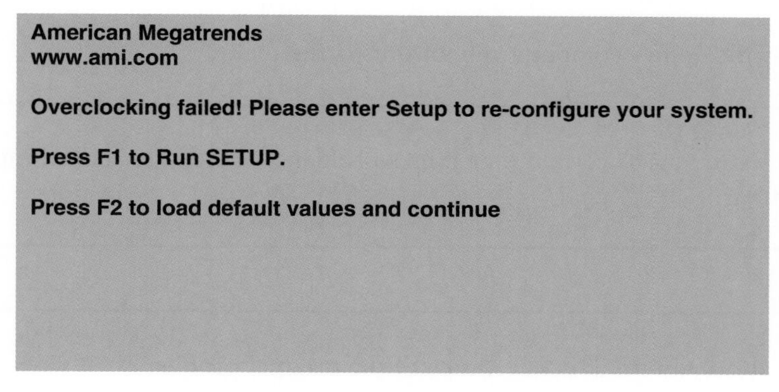

Figure 1-3 John's system hangs early in the boot and displays this screen

3. John knows he has not overclocked his system and does not want to use BIOS default settings unless he has no other option. He presses F1 and the system enters CMOS setup.
4. In CMOS setup, he notices the date and time are correct and exits without saving changes. The Windows XP desktop loads normally. In the lower-right corner of the screen, he sees the bubble shown in Figure 1-4.

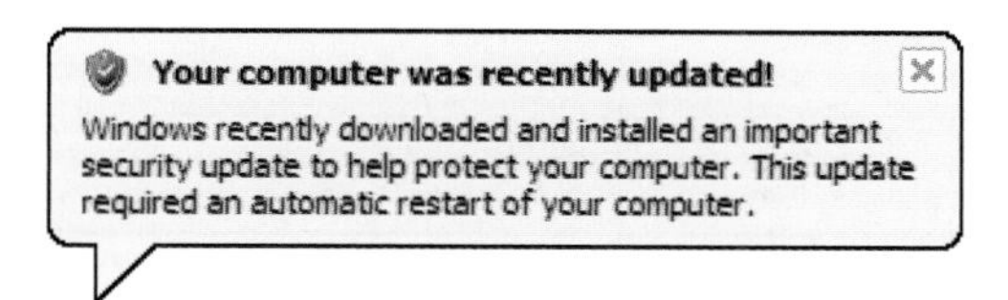

Figure 1-4 This bubble appeared on the Windows desktop

5. John is not satisfied that all is well, so he reboots the system. As the startup BIOS performs POST, he hears a single beep followed by two beeps, and the Windows desktop again loads normally.
6. John looks up the beep codes in AMI documentation and finds that one, two, and three beeps are all memory-related errors.
7. He powers down the system and reseats the two memory modules. As a preventive measure, he uses a can of compressed air to blow dust out of the case. And, because he suspects he might later need to replace the DIMMs, he records this information printed on each DIMM:

   Elixir 256 MB DDR-400 MHz CL3 PC3200
8. He replaces the front panel and side panel of the PC case and powers up the system. When he does, the monitor screen is totally blank and he hears no beeps. He does hear the fans spinning.
9. He powers down the system again, reseats the DIMMs again, replaces the front panel, and powers up the system. The system boots to the Windows desktop.
10. John decides to perform a memory test using third-party memory testing software. Memory failed the first test, but when he tried it a second time, memory passed with no errors.

TROUBLESHOOTING

Answer the following questions about what John did, the source of the problem(s), and what to do next.

- Why did John's computer reboot during the night?

  ____

- How can you be certain that John's problem is hardware related rather than software related?

  ____

  ____

- What do you think is the source of the original problem?

  ____

- In Step 4, John discovers the date and time are correct. What does this indicate?

  ____

- In Step 8, why do you think the monitor was blank?

  ____

- What are four things you would suggest that John do next? List in the order John should do them.

  ____

  ____

  ____

  ____

The motherboard documentation does not normally contain the beep codes needed for troubleshooting, but you should be able to download them from the BIOS manufacturer Web site.

- What is the name of the document that contains the explanation of beep codes downloaded from the AMI Web site?

  ____

- Using the Internet as your source, list the names and Web sites of two diagnostic software applications that can test memory.

  ____

  ____

For more troubleshooting practice, answer this question about a PC problem:

- Mary complains that the window shown in Figure 1-5 appears each time she restarts her PC. She does not use a RAID controller even though her motherboard has that feature. How can you prevent the window from appearing without installing the controller in Windows?

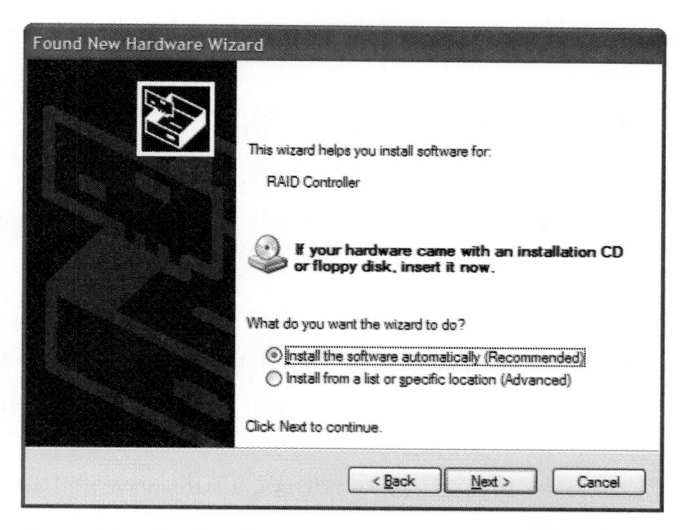

Figure 1-5 The Found New Hardware wizard is attempting to install a RAID controller

REVIEW QUESTIONS

1. In troubleshooting a boot problem, what is the advantage of restoring all CMOS settings to their default values?

 ____

2. In troubleshooting a boot problem, what is the disadvantage of restoring all CMOS settings to their default values?

 ____

3. In troubleshooting a boot problem, what is the advantage of disabling the quick boot feature in CMOS setup?

 ____

4. What is the MHz rating of a memory module that is rated at PC2100?

 ____

5. To take advantage of dual channeling, what is the minimum number of DIMM DDR modules that need to be installed?

 ____

PRACTICE EXAM

The following practice exam covers the domain *Personal Computer Components*. Answers to the odd-numbered questions are provided in Appendix B.

1. You are upgrading a desktop computer that has a motherboard that supports PATA ATA/66, dual channeling using DDR DIMMs, and USB 2.0. Which component cannot be installed in this system or will install without its full functionality?

 a. hard drive using the ultra DMA/66 standard

 b. CD-ROM drive with a SATA interface

c. 240-pin DIMMs

d. Wireless USB adapter

2. Which statement about installing DIMMs is true?

a. DIMMs must be installed in matching pairs.

b. 240-pin and 184-pin DIMMs can be installed on the same motherboard.

c. All DIMMs must match in speed.

d. Notches on the DIMM must match notches in the memory slot.

3. Which statement about installing a hard drive using a SATA interface is true?

a. If the hard drive has a PATA connector, you can use a PATA-to-SATA adapter to connect it to the SATA interface.

b. The SATA cable accommodates two drives, a hard drive and an optical drive.

c. The hard drive DIP switch must be set to master.

d. Two power cords must be connected to the hard drive.

4. A user tells you that her Windows XP system crashes occasionally. When you arrive at her site, you notice the room is especially hot. What can you do to prevent the system from overheating? Choose *two* answers:

a. Remove the stacks of books and papers surrounding the monitor vents.

b. Suggest to the user she lower the temperature in the room, so that the system will not overheat.

c. Defrag the hard drive to improve computer performance.

d. Install a bay cover over the empty bay on the front of the PC case.

5. A user tells you that his mechanical mouse does not always work. It is difficult to move around on the screen and sometimes halts. Which action is most likely to solve the problem?

a. Exchange the mouse battery.

b. Update the mouse drivers.

c. Clean the mouse rollers using a cotton swab and a small amount of liquid soap.

d. Clean the mouse rollers using compressed air.

6. What is the storage capacity of a single-sided, single-layer DVD-R disc?

a. 4.7 GB

b. 8.5 GB

c. 9.4 GB

d. 17 GB

7. What is the bandwidth of a PCI bus that is 32 bits wide and is clocked at 33 MHz?

a. 33 MB/sec

b. 133 MB/sec

c. 256 MB/sec

d. 1,056 MB/sec

8. USB 2.0 is how many times faster than USB 1.1?
   a. 10 times faster.
   b. 40 times faster.
   c. 60 times faster.
   d. 100 times faster.
9. A user needs to have redundant data storage to assure that data is not lost as the data is being input. Which type of RAID implementation supports this drive imaging?
   a. RAID 0
   b. RAID 1
   c. RAID 5
   d. RAID 6
10. Which statement is true about video adapter interfaces to the motherboard?
    a. AGP 2x is twice as fast as PCI Express x2.
    b. AGP 8x is faster than PCI Express x16.
    c. PCI Express x16 is faster than AGP 8x.
    d. Most motherboards have one AGP slot and one PCI Express slot.
11. A CD-ROM drive is beginning to skip when playing music CDs. What is the best way to fix the problem?
    a. Replace the drive. CD-ROM drives typically cannot be fixed once they start giving errors.
    b. Use an optical drive cleaning kit to clean the drive.
    c. Use a soft cloth and denatured alcohol to clean inside the drive.
    d. Use compressed air to blow inside the drive.
12. When should you *not* wear an ESD bracelet?
    a. When working inside a desktop computer.
    b. When disassembling a laptop computer.
    c. When installing memory on a desktop.
    d. When working inside a CRT monitor.
13. You install a second hard drive in the system. When you first turn on the system, you can hear the drives spinning, but BIOS does not recognize either drive. What is likely the problem?
    a. You need to use an 80-conductor cable rather than a 40-conductor cable.
    b. The new drive is too large for BIOS to recognize. You need to flash BIOS.
    c. The IDE cable is faulty.
    d. The jumpers on the two drives are not set correctly.
14. Which OS utility is most likely to improve performance in a Windows XP system?
    a. Chkdsk
    b. Scandisk

c. Defrag

d. Diskpart

15. When you first turn on a system, you can hear fans turn on and the hard drive is spinning. You see nothing on the monitor screen although the LED light on the monitor indicates it is turned on. What should you do first?

    a. Check the power cord connections to the computer case and the outlet.

    b. Open the case and check the power connector to the motherboard.

    c. Replace the motherboard.

    d. Check the power-on switch on the back of the computer case.

CHAPTER 2

Laptops and Portable Devices

Troubleshooting scenarios in this chapter:

- **Scenario 2.1:** Use Notebook Display Options and the Fn Key
- **Scenario 2.2:** Replace the LCD Panel Field Replaceable Units
- **Scenario 2.3:** Manage Power Saving Options
- **Scenario 2.4:** Use Notebook Diagnostic Software

SUMMARY OF DOMAIN CONTENT

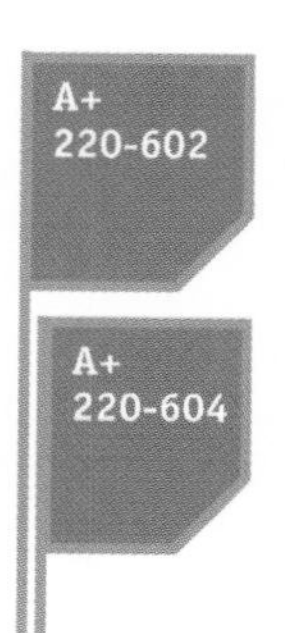

This section of the chapter contains a summary overview of the content in the CompTIA A+ 220-602 and 220-604 combined objectives for Domain 2, *Laptops and Portable Devices*. Please note that the A+ 220-603 exam does not include the *Laptops and Portable Devices* domain. The high-level objectives for this domain are:

- Identify fundamental principles of using laptops and portable devices
- Install, configure, optimize and upgrade laptops and portable devices
- Use tools, diagnostic procedures and troubleshooting techniques for laptops and portable devices

IDENTIFY FUNDAMENTAL PRINCIPLES OF USING LAPTOPS AND PORTABLE DEVICES

Identify appropriate applications for laptop-specific communication connections such as Bluetooth, infrared, cellular WAN and Ethernet

Bluetooth, infrared, and proprietary wireless technologies are used for short-range connections such as between a notebook and a PDA, printer, or mouse. Infrared is older than Bluetooth and has the disadvantage that the device and notebook must be in the line-of-sight of each other with no obstructions. Bluetooth transmits at 3 Mbps, compared to 11 Mbps and 54 Mbps for WiFi, and Bluetooth encrypts data for security. Cellular WAN is used to connect a notebook to the Internet by way of a cellular phone network. Ethernet is a wired network technology that uses CAT5, CAT5e, and CAT6 cabling. An Ethernet port looks like a telephone port, but wider.

Identify appropriate laptop-specific power and electrical input devices and determine how amperage and voltage can affect performance

Notebooks can be powered by an AC adapter, a DC adapter, or a battery pack. Connect the AC adapter with the battery pack installed to recharge the battery pack. Some AC adapters can switch between 110 V and 220 V AC power. Current battery packs use a Lithium Ion battery, and older battery packs used a Nickel Metal Hydride (NiMH) battery. Keep more than one battery pack available and charged when working in remote locations. Typical batteries have a 40 watt-hour rating. For a battery to keep its charge longer, use one with a higher watt-hour rating. To conserve power when using a battery pack, a notebook might reduce LCD panel brightness. To further conserve power, a notebook uses standby mode and hibernation when not in use. In standby mode, a notebook's hard drive, monitor, and processor are turned off. In hibernation, everything in RAM is copied to a file on the hard drive and then the system shuts down.

Identify the major components of the LCD including inverter, screen and video card

Some high-end notebooks contain a video card with embedded memory. All notebooks have an LCD screen (also called an LCD panel), which uses an inverter card that controls voltage to the screen. A notebook with video problems might need the video card, LCD screen, or inverter replaced. Replacing the LCD screen is expensive and might cost more than the value of the notebook.

INSTALL, CONFIGURE, OPTIMIZE AND UPGRADE LAPTOPS AND PORTABLE DEVICES

Demonstrate the safe removal of laptop-specific hardware such as peripherals, hot-swappable and non-hot-swappable devices

- Ports and slots used to connect peripheral devices include 16-bit PCMCIA slot (legacy), PC Card slot, CardBus slot, ExpressCard slot, USB port (USB 1.1 or USB 2.0), FireWire port, Ethernet port, modem port, various audio ports, Secure Digital (SD) slot, CompactFlash Card slot, 15-pin VGA video port, and power jack for DC or AC power adapter.
- PCMCIA slots come in three sizes: Type I, II, and III, with each slot wider than the previous slot to accommodate a thicker card. A Type III slot can hold a portable disk drive or two Type I or Type II cards.
- CardBus is an improved 32-bit version of the older 16-bit PC Card slot. ExpressCard slots use PCI Express technology and come in two sizes: ExpressCard/34 and ExpressCard/54.
- Before removing a hot-swappable PC Card or ExpressCard device, first stop the card service. You can then remove the device without shutting down the system. Non-hot-swappable devices such as a memory module or a Mini-PCI card must be connected or disconnected while the system is shut down.
- When upgrading memory on a notebook, only use memory modules approved by the notebook manufacturer and know that some manufacturers use proprietary modules.

Describe how video sharing affects memory upgrades

Video sharing refers to the video system using regular RAM for video data rather than using dedicated video RAM. Video sharing results in less RAM being available for Windows and applications and might require that you install additional RAM.

USE TOOLS, DIAGNOSTIC PROCEDURES AND TROUBLESHOOTING TECHNIQUES FOR LAPTOPS AND PORTABLE DEVICES

Use procedures and techniques to diagnose power conditions, video, keyboard, pointer and wireless card issues for example:

- *Verify AC power (e.g., LEDs, swap AC adapter)*
  Verify power is available by looking for lights on the notebook and listening for the fan running. Check all AC adapter connectors, and verify the power outlet is working. Check the LED light on the AC adapter; exchange the AC adapter. If power is still not getting to the system, most likely the problem is the motherboard.
- *Verify DC power*
  A DC adapter provides power to a notebook from a car or truck power outlet. Verify an AC or DC adapter is good by looking for lights on the notebook, checking all connections, verifying the outlet is providing power, and exchanging the DC adapter.

- ***Remove unneeded peripherals***
  Reduce the system to essentials to eliminate any problems caused by peripherals and to isolate the problem. Unplug USB devices, external monitor, printer, keyboard, or mouse, and disconnect PC Card and PCI Express devices. Troubleshoot the system with only essential components installed.
- ***Plug in external monitor***
  When the display screen is blank, try using an external monitor. If the external monitor works, you have isolated the problem to the LCD panel assembly. If the external monitor does not work, the problem might be related to the motherboard, CPU, power, or memory. After you plug in the monitor, use the Fn key and a function key on the keyboard to activate the monitor.
- ***Toggle Fn keys***
  Often the Fn key is used along with other function keys to control external monitors, power features such as hibernation, LCD panel brightness, and other notebook features.
- ***Check LCD cutoff switch***
  If the LCD panel is blank, the switch that directs all display to an external monitor might be turned off.
- ***Verify backlight functionality and pixilation***
  LCD panel backlighting and pixilation is controlled by the inverter. Use keys on the keyboard to adjust backlighting. Use the Display Properties window to control resolution and pixilation. To prevent fuzzy graphics, use the native resolution of a notebook LCD panel.
- ***Stylus issues (e.g., digitizer problems)***
  Tablet PCs and PDAs use a stylus for touch screen input. A stylus looks much like a pencil. To protect the touch screen, only use a stylus recommended by the product manufacturer. A stylus does not work on a laptop touchpad, which only works with a finger touch.
- ***Unique laptop keypad issues***
  Some notebooks don't have a keypad, but do have a way to toggle a group of keys near the right side of the keyboard from letters to numbers. You can also purchase an external USB keypad.
- ***Antenna wires***
  Notebook antenna wires are usually embedded inside the notebook case. Some antennas are embedded inside the LCD panel; raising the panel to full upright position might improve the wireless signal.

SCENARIO 2.1: USE NOTEBOOK DISPLAY OPTIONS AND THE FN KEY

OBJECTIVES

The goal of this lab is to help you learn how to support notebook video. Support technicians are often called on to support a variety of computers and peripherals; therefore, it's important to learn to use more than one type of notebook. If possible, perform this lab using more than one type of notebook. After completing this lab, you will be able to:

- Use Display Properties to change display settings.
- Use an external monitor or video projector.
- Communicate with difficult users.

MATERIALS REQUIRED

This lab requires the following:

- Notebook computer
- External monitor or projector

LAB PREPARATION

Before the lab begins, the instructor or lab assistant needs to do the following:

- Verify the notebook computer and external video device are available and working.

SCENARIO BACKGROUND

PC support technicians often find themselves needing to respond to emergencies created by the lack of preparation by others. As you respond to these types of technical challenges, experience helps! Good communication is also needed to help calm nervous users in desperate situations.

ESTIMATED COMPLETION TIME: 1 hour

SCENARIO

Sharon has worked for two weeks to put together a PowerPoint presentation to support her important speech to the executives in her company. The presentation is scheduled for 9:00 this Friday morning. On Monday, she requests a projector in the conference room by Thursday afternoon, so that she'll have plenty of time to make sure all is working before people start to arrive around 8:45 on Friday morning. Late Thursday evening, she puts the finishing touches on the presentation and prints 25 copies, more than enough for the expected 20 attendees. She arrives at work about 8:00 a.m. the next day and heads for the conference room to hook up her notebook to the video projector. So far, so good.

But when she arrives in the conference room with printouts, notebook, and coffee in hand, she finds no projector! She calls technical support (that's you) to fix the problem. You, too, have just arrived at work and are busy making yourself a cup of coffee when you answer the phone to hear an angry, frantic user tell you in no uncertain terms you've screwed up and need to get down here immediately with a projector. You don't recall ever receiving her request.

- What do you say on the phone and what questions do you ask?

____

____

____

____

____

TROUBLESHOOTING

You find a projector and bring it to the conference room. Sharon has powered up her Windows XP notebook and opened the PowerPoint presentation. She turns her back to you as you set the projector down, making it clear to you that she is not in a friendly mood. You turn to leave the room. "Wait!" Sharon says, "Aren't you going to connect it?" In your organization, you know that users are expected to manage their own projectors and laptops for these presentations. Obviously, Sharon is not technically prepared.

- With only 15 minutes before the presentation starts, what do you say and do?

  ____

  ____

- List below the steps to connect the projector and set up the display so that PowerPoint is displayed on Sharon's notebook and also on the projector. (In a lab environment where you don't have a projector, use a monitor to practice these steps.)

  ____

  ____

  ____

  ____

  ____

> **Note**
>
> When connecting a notebook to a projector, know that the projector must support the screen resolution used by the notebook. If the projector shows a blank screen, try a different screen resolution setting on the notebook.

- On your particular notebook, what key do you use along with the Fn key to toggle the display between video devices?

  ____

- For your notebook, list other keys that can be used along with the Fn key and the purpose of each keystroke combination.

  ____

  ____

  ____

  ____

  ____

  ____

  ____

  ____

- If Sharon pauses too long during the presentation, the screen saver might activate and cause the screen to go blank or the system might go into standby mode. How do you set the power options and display settings so these interruptions to the presentation won't happen?

Sharon decides she needs her Windows desktop available on the notebook's screen at the same time the PowerPoint presentation is displayed on the projector, but she has no clue how to do this.

- List the steps to make this adjustment.

Throughout this entire ordeal, Sharon has yet to say anything friendly or positive to you, not even one word of thanks. Your anger is growing, but so far you've kept your cool. Executives begin to fill the room. Nervously, Sharon notices more than 20 people are present, and it's still only five minutes to nine. She turns to you and sheepishly asks, "Would you do me a favor? Please make me 10 more copies of this presentation."

- How do you respond?

REVIEW QUESTIONS

1. Listen as another student reads his or her communication on the phone with the user as written down earlier in this lab. Is this student communicating well, being a good listener, and doing his or her best to calm the user and respond appropriately? Ask the other student to comment on your conversation with the user and record his or her comments below.

2. In Question 1 above, based on the other student's comments, how can you improve your communication skills?

3. Notebooks vary in the key combination used to toggle video. Without having a user manual available, describe how you would figure out which key combination to use on a notebook.

4. In the Display Properties window, what tab is used to extend the Windows desktop onto the external monitor?

____

5. When troubleshooting an LCD panel that is giving problems or is blank, how can using an external monitor help you?

____

SCENARIO 2.2: REPLACE THE LCD PANEL FIELD REPLACEABLE UNITS

OBJECTIVES

The goal of this lab is to help you troubleshoot hardware problems with a notebook's LCD panel. After completing this lab, you will be able to:

- Identify hardware problems with the LCD panel.
- Replace LCD panel components.

MATERIALS REQUIRED

This lab requires the following:

- A notebook computer that can be disassembled
- The notebook's technical reference manual that contains instructions for disassembly
- Internet access on this or another computer

LAB PREPARATION

Before the lab begins, the instructor or lab assistant needs to do the following:

- Provide each student or workgroup with a notebook computer that can be disassembled and its technical reference manual.
- Verify Internet access is available.

SCENARIO BACKGROUND

The A+ exams require that you know about replacing a few internal notebook components. Computer components that field technicians are expected to be able to replace are called field replaceable units (FRUs). The internal FRUs for a notebook computer might include the hard drive, memory, optical drive, floppy drive, LCD panel assembly, Mini PCI card, motherboard, CPU, keyboard, PC Card socket, sound card, and battery pack. Depending on the notebook, the LCD panel assembly FRU might be the entire LCD assembly or the individual parts, which are the LCD panel itself, the inverter, and the video card (if one is present).

Be very careful when disassembling a notebook. The case and parts are often made of plastic and easily broken or marred when too much pressure or force is applied.

Notebook computers vary drastically in the way they are assembled and disassembled. As a PC support technician, you are not required to know how to disassemble every brand and model of notebook. However, if you have a technical reference manual that includes the steps to disassemble a notebook to replace a component, you should be able to do the job. This lab gives you that information and experience. This lab uses an IBM ThinkPad X20. However, you will most likely use a different notebook with its own reference manual.

ESTIMATED COMPLETION TIME: 3 hours

SCENARIO

Joseph brings you his notebook computer complaining that it is dead, and asks you to repair it. Before you service any notebook, always ask these questions:

1. Does it hold important data not backed up?
2. What recently happened?
3. What must I do to reproduce the problem?
4. Is the notebook under warranty?

In asking these four questions, you find out the notebook does hold important data and that it is not under warranty. You also find out that Joseph allowed a coworker to carry his notebook from one building to another along with a bunch of other computers and components. Joseph suspects the coworker was not careful when handling the notebook. The first time Joseph turned on the notebook after this move, he found it "dead."

TROUBLESHOOTING

You're now ready to investigate the problem. You plug in the notebook, turn it on, and make these observations:

- The LCD panel appears blank, but the notebook is not "dead." The keyboard lights are lit and you hear the sound of the fan when you first turn on the computer.
- You look very carefully at the LCD panel and notice a faint display that you cannot read.

You next try to use the keys to increase the LCD panel brightness. Even when you have increased the brightness as far as possible, you still can't read what's on the screen. Next, you plug in an external monitor and use the appropriate keys to direct video output to this device. You can now read the display on the external monitor.

- What is the next very important thing you should do?

____

You're now ready to discuss the repairs with Joseph. The notebook does not use a video card, so the two FRUs that apply to video are the LCD panel and the inverter. It is likely a damaged inverter is causing the dim display. However, you make sure that Joseph understands the entire LCD panel might need replacing. The price of the inverter is minimal compared to the value of the notebook. However, because the notebook is several years old, you suspect that replacing the LCD panel will cost more than the notebook is worth. Research and answer these questions:

- What is the brand and model of your notebook?

  ____

- What is the price of the video inverter? Print the Web page supporting your answer.

  ____

- What is the price of the LCD panel? Print the Web page supporting your answer.

  ____

- What is the value of this notebook? Determining the value of a notebook can be a little difficult and is usually a best guess. Try searching auction sites such as eBay.com for a match or near match.

  ____

- What sources of information did you use to determine the value of the notebook?

  ____

Caution

Be careful as you work. Many parts are plastic and are fragile. If you force them, they might snap or break.

After discussing the price of components and his options, Joseph decides to have you try replacing the inverter. If that doesn't solve the problem, then he plans to buy a new notebook.

After purchasing the inverter, you're ready to replace this component. Listed below are the steps to replace the inverter in the ThinkPad X20. The steps for your notebook will vary.

1. Power down the notebook, unplug it, and remove the battery.
2. Following directions in the technical reference manual, the next step is to remove the keyboard. Remove four screws on the bottom of the notebook. These four screws are marked by two triangles imprinted beside each screw. Be sure to keep removed screws well organized and labeled so you will later be able to put the right screws in the right holes when you reassemble.
3. Push up on the keyboard from the bottom and carefully lift the keyboard out of the cavity as shown in Figure 2-1.

Figure 2-1 Lift up on the keyboard to remove it

4. Remove the keyboard ribbon cable from the notebook so you can lift the keyboard out and place it out of your way. See Figure 2-2. Don't stack components as you remove them.

Figure 2-2 Disconnect the keyboard cable and then remove the keyboard

5. You're now ready to remove the LCD assembly. Begin by removing two screws on the back of the notebook near the LCD panel hinges. Next, remove the hinge covers. You can then remove the two screws holding the LCD panel to the notebook. As shown in Figure 2-3, disconnect the video ribbon cable from the notebook and lift the LCD panel from the notebook.

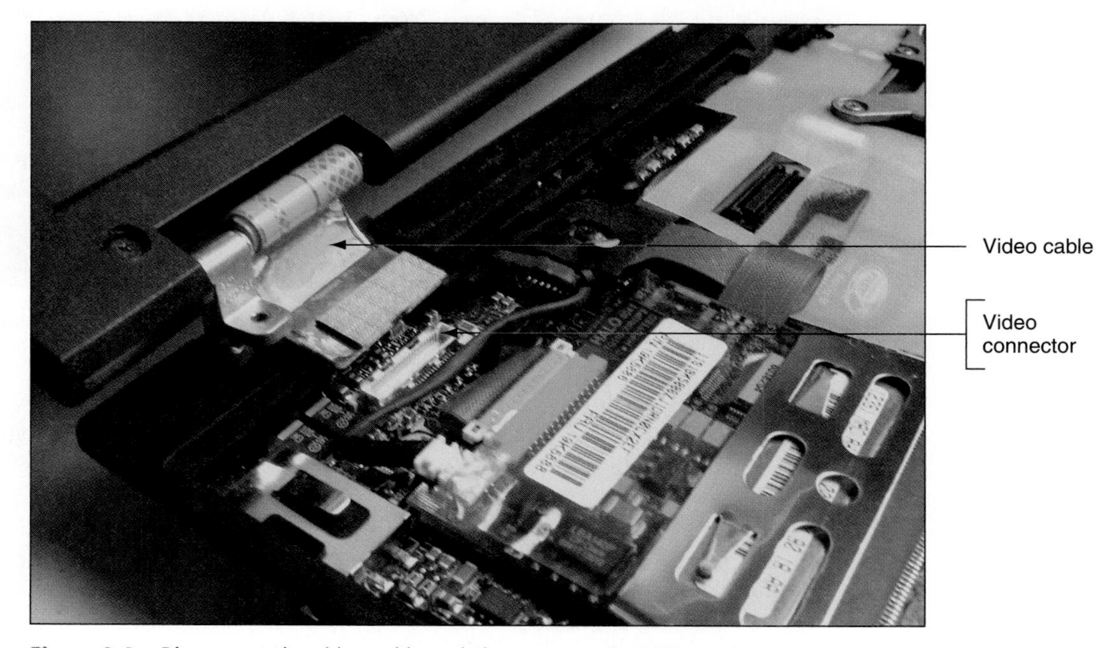

Figure 2-3 Disconnect the video cable and then remove the LCD panel

6. By removing the screws along the sides and bottom of the LCD panel assembly, you can carefully lift the LCD panel out of its enclosure to expose the inverter as shown in Figure 2-4. Also shown in the figure is the new inverter. Before proceeding, make sure your new component will fit the space and the connectors match. This new inverter is not an exact match, but it does fit.

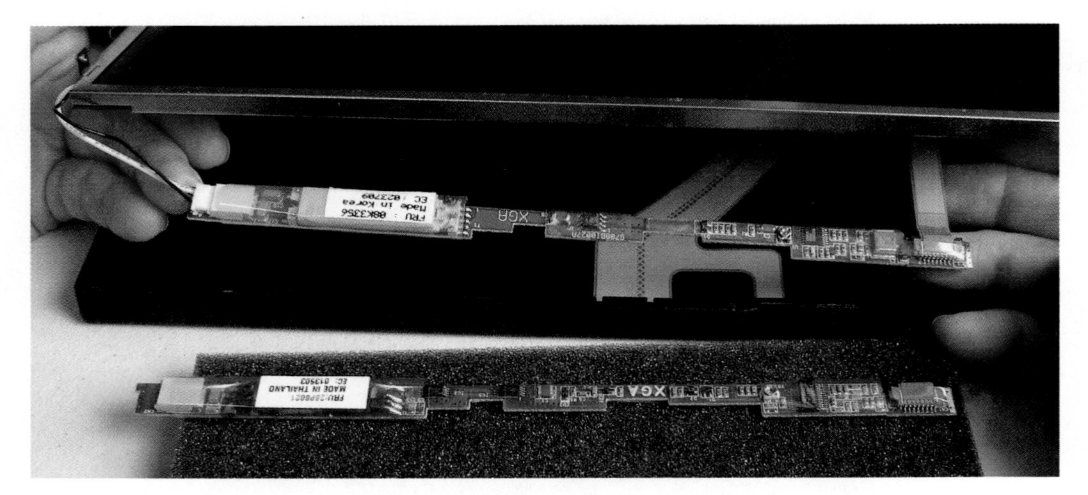

Figure 2-4 The inverter is exposed and is compared to the new one

7. Disconnect the old inverter and install the new one. When disconnecting the ribbon cable from the old inverter, notice you must first lift up on the lock holding the ZIF connector in place as shown in Figure 2-5.

Figure 2-5 Lift up on the ZIF connector locking mechanism before removing the ribbon cable

8. Install the new inverter.
9. Reassemble the LCD panel assembly. Make sure the assembly is put together with a tight fit so that all screws line up well.
10. Reattach the LCD panel assembly to the notebook.
11. Replace the keyboard and replace the four screws on the bottom of the notebook holding the keyboard in place.
12. Plug in the AC adapter and power up the notebook.

In a lab environment, disassemble your notebook to the point that you remove the inverter from the notebook. Then reinstall the inverter and reassemble the notebook. List below the key steps you took to disassemble your notebook, uninstall and reinstall the inverter, and return the notebook to working order:

When you power up the notebook, to your disappointment, you discover the display is still dim. You now know most likely the LCD panel itself was damaged in the move. After talking with Joseph, you remind him that he can still use the notebook as long as he uses an external monitor for display.

REVIEW QUESTIONS

1. What are the three FRUs of the video subsystem?

2. Of the three video FRUs, which one is optional?

3. When replacing the LCD panel on any notebook, is it always necessary to first remove the hard drive?

4. To protect the user's investments in time and money, before disassembling a notebook, what two very important questions should a technician always ask the user?

____

5. Generally, which is the more expensive notebook component, an LCD panel or an inverter?

____

SCENARIO 2.3: MANAGE POWER SAVING OPTIONS

OBJECTIVES

The goal of this lab is to help you learn to manage a notebook's power saving options and help users manage their notebook power. After completing this lab, you will be able to:

- Manage notebook power saving features.
- Troubleshoot power problems.

MATERIALS REQUIRED

This lab requires the following:

- A working notebook computer
- Internet access on this or another computer

LAB PREPARATION

Before the lab begins, the instructor or lab assistant needs to do the following:

- Verify that a working notebook is available for each student or workgroup.
- Verify that Internet access is available.

SCENARIO BACKGROUND

Notebooks are often used where AC power is not available. It's a good idea to know how to best manage power so that the battery pack charge will last as long as possible. A PC support technician also needs to know how to troubleshoot problems with power. In this lab, you learn about these skills as well as how to help users with power problems.

ESTIMATED COMPLETION TIME: 1 hour

SCENARIOS AND TROUBLESHOOTING

You work at a customer service center for notebook computers. Lucia comes in complaining that her Fujitsu N6220 Windows XP notebook battery pack needs recharging far too often.

1. What questions should you ask to try to get to the bottom of the problem?

____

____

2. After talking with Lucia, you decide to check how her notebook is configured to manage power, so you check the power management options in Windows. Using your notebook computer as an example, answer these questions:
   - How did you access the Power Options Properties window?
   - What is a second way to access the Power Options Properties window?
   - How much disk space does your notebook require when it goes into hibernation?
   - Explain the difference between standby and hibernation.
   - What is the disadvantage of always using hibernation over standby when you are not using your notebook?
   - What are the steps to cause the power management icon to display in the taskbar?
   - What power options are available on your notebook when you press the power button?
   - What power options are available on your notebook when you close the lid?
   - What is the purpose of the Presentation Power Scheme?
3. You explain to Lucia that she can dim the brightness of the LCD panel to conserve power. On your notebook, how do you control the LCD panel brightness?
4. Lucia wants the power options to work so that when she presses the power button, the system goes into hibernation. How do you make this adjustment?

5. You test the adjustment by pressing the power button, but nothing happens. You suspect that the power button might have been disabled in CMOS setup. How do you access CMOS setup on your notebook?

 ____

6. Search CMOS setup for an option to enable or disable the power button. Does your setup contain this option? If so, on what menu?

 ____

7. In talking with Lucia, you discover she spends a lot of time traveling and would benefit from having a second battery pack available. Search the Internet and print a Web page showing the price of a battery pack for your notebook.

 ____

Jason comes to your service counter telling you that his notebook power has failed. Sometimes users might conclude that a problem is caused by one component when it is really caused by another. Follow these steps to troubleshoot the notebook:

1. Plug in the AC adapter and turn on the power to the notebook. Nothing appears on the LCD panel, but you notice the lights on the front of the notebook are lit, including the power indicator light (LED). You conclude that the problem might be caused by a faulty AC adapter, RAM, the motherboard, or the LCD panel.
2. To eliminate the LCD panel, you plug in an external monitor and try to direct video to the monitor. The monitor does not receive a signal. What is your conclusion about video?

 ____

3. By reseating RAM, you do not totally eliminate RAM as the source of the problem, but reseating RAM might solve the problem.
 - List the steps to reseat RAM:

 ____

 ____

 ____

 - Why is it important to unplug the AC adapter and remove the battery pack as the first steps before you reseat RAM?

 ____

 ____

 ____

4. Check that the AC adapter is connected at all points and that the power outlet is working. How can you test the power outlet?

 ____

5. Your shop keeps some known-good test components available for these kinds of situations. Therefore, you next try replacing the AC adapter with a known-good one and the memory modules with known-good modules. The problem does not go

away. The next component to replace is the motherboard, but this is a complex procedure and requires the customer to first agree to the expense. What is the price of the motherboard for your system? Print the Web page supporting your answer.

____

6. What is the value of your notebook? Print the Web page supporting your answer. Do you think the repair job is a good investment?

____

REVIEW QUESTIONS

1. Why is it important to remove peripheral devices such as an external USB device or external mouse before troubleshooting a power problem on a notebook?

____

2. Which do you think requires more power, using a DVD to play a movie on a notebook or typing a Word document?

____

3. If you configure Windows on a notebook to hibernate after 30 minutes of inactivity, but the notebook remains fully functioning, what might be the problem?

____

4. If a notebook has two internal hard drives, can you decide on which drive the hibernation information will be saved or must it always go to drive C?

____

5. If video output does not work to the external monitor, why can you conclude that the problem is not the LCD panel?

____

SCENARIO 2.4: USE NOTEBOOK DIAGNOSTIC SOFTWARE

OBJECTIVES

The goal of this lab is to help you learn to research and use diagnostic software to troubleshoot problems with notebook computers. After completing this lab, you will be able to:

- Research and use diagnostic software on a notebook computer.
- Research replacing a part on a notebook.

MATERIALS REQUIRED

This lab requires the following:

- A working notebook computer
- Internet access on this or another computer

LAB PREPARATION

Before the lab begins, the instructor or lab assistant needs to do the following:

- Verify that a working notebook is available for each student or workgroup.
- Verify that Internet access is available.

SCENARIO BACKGROUND

Servicing notebooks is different from servicing desktop systems in many respects. One difference is that because notebooks are more proprietary in design, you are more dependent on tools and manuals provided by the notebook manufacturer than with desktops. Some manufacturers provide excellent service manuals that you can download from their Web sites and others keep this information more private.

Many notebook manufacturers store diagnostic software on a notebook that can be accessed at startup. This software can be used to test key hardware components and can be useful when troubleshooting a notebook. In this lab, you learn about service manuals, diagnostic software, and other tools that are available and how to access and use them.

ESTIMATED COMPLETION TIME: 1 hour

SCENARIO AND TROUBLESHOOTING

You run a small PC repair shop, and Janice comes in with a notebook computer that has been dropped. The notebook is an HP Pavilion ze4145 with model number F4893H that is not under warranty. She tells you that she thinks the entire computer is useless because it appeared "dead" when she turned it on. She's especially upset over data on the hard drive that she believes has been lost.

- After you fill out the customer intake form, you are now ready to face the problem. List the first three things you should do to try to save the data and troubleshoot the problem:

  ____

  ____

  ____

- After you plug in the AC adapter and turn on the laptop, you discover the lights on the notebook are lit and you hear the fan running, but the LCD panel is blank. When you connect an external monitor, you see the Windows XP logon screen. Janice breathes a sign of relief. What do you do now?

  ____

- You suspect the LCD panel is broken, but you decide it would be a good idea to run hardware diagnostic software to check for other hardware problems. Diagnostic software is written specifically for a particular brand notebook, and is often stored in a hidden utility partition on the hard drive or on the recovery CD that comes with the notebook. The software is accessed by pressing a key at startup or by booting from a recovery CD. Also know that, for some notebooks, the diagnostic software in the hidden partition is disabled by default and must be enabled in CMOS setup before you can use it.

- Most notebook manufacturers provide diagnostic software hidden on the hard drive that is accessed at startup by pressing a certain key. Do the following to find out about diagnostic software and how to use it:

  1. Go to the Hewlett-Packard (HP) Web site (*www.hp.com*) and download the service manual for this notebook. What is the name of the downloaded PDF file?

     ____

  2. What key do you press at startup to access the diagnostic software stored on this notebook?

     ____

  3. What two types of tests can you run using the e-DiagTools software?

     ____

  4. If the hard drive is broken, what other method can you use to run the e-DiagTools software?

     ____

  5. After you repair this notebook, what three types of tests does HP recommend you run to verify the repair?

     ____

     ____

     ____

- Based on the information in the service manual, what is the part number of the LCD panel?

  ____

- What is the price of the LCD panel if you buy it from the HP Web site?

  ____

- Research the service manual and list the high-level steps to replace the LCD panel.

  ____

  ____

  ____

  ____

  ____

- Before you commit to replacing a notebook's internal component, you need to be confident that you have enough information and directions to open the notebook, access the part, and reassemble the notebook. Do you think you have enough information to do the repair? Why or why not?

◢ If you don't think you have enough information, what is your next step?

HP offers excellent diagnostic software, but not all notebook manufacturers do that. Also, HP makes its notebook service manuals available on the Web, but many notebook manufacturers only release their service manuals to authorized service centers. For these service manuals, you can sometimes use an Internet search engine to find them posted to other sites. Using your lab notebook, available documentation for the notebook, and the Internet, answer these questions:

1. What is the brand and model of your notebook? What is the Web site of your notebook manufacturer?

2. Can you obtain the service manual for your notebook? If so, what Web site or other source did you use?

3. Does your notebook have diagnostic software? If so, how is it accessed? List all methods.

4. If you have diagnostic software, how does this software compare to the HP e-DiagTools software?

5. If you have diagnostic software, run it using as thorough a test as the software offers. List the results of the test.

REVIEW QUESTIONS

1. What document for a notebook contains technical troubleshooting procedures, part numbers, and instructions for disassembly?

2. Why would you want to run diagnostic software after you have repaired a notebook and verified the repaired component does work?

3. Before you purchase an internal notebook part to replace a broken one, what should you verify?

4. If your service manual tells you to press F12 at startup to run diagnostic software, but nothing happens when you press F12, what do you do next?

5. List three troubleshooting situations where diagnostic software might be useful.

PRACTICE EXAM

The following practice exam covers the domain *Laptop and Portable Devices*. Answers to the odd-numbered questions are provided in Appendix B.

1. Which of the following actions are likely to be accomplished using the Fn key in combination with a function key? Choose *two* answers:
   - **a.** Change the brightness of the LCD panel.
   - **b.** Power up the system.
   - **c.** Put the system into hibernation.
   - **d.** Eject a PC Card from its slot.
2. You boot a laptop and discover that the LCD panel shows a very faint display. What is the next thing you should do?
   - **a.** Try using an external monitor.
   - **b.** Reboot the laptop.
   - **c.** Increase the brightness level of the display.
   - **d.** Replace the LCD panel assembly.
3. Which wireless standard is most likely to be used to connect a PDA to a laptop?
   - **a.** USB 2.0
   - **b.** Bluetooth
   - **c.** 802.11n
   - **d.** Infrared

4. Which of the following devices are not hot-swappable on a laptop?

   a. Modem PC Card

   b. Battery pack

   c. Flash drive

   d. Wireless Mini PCI card

5. Which types of connections can be used to connect a laptop to the Internet? Choose *two* answers.

   a. IEEE 1284

   b. Cellular WAN PC Card

   c. 802.11g

   d. Infrared

6. A laptop has one DIMM module that holds 256 MB of RAM. The laptop onboard video uses 64 MB of shared video RAM. You upgrade memory by installing a second DIMM that holds 256 MB of RAM. How much total memory is now available to the operating system?

   a. 512 MB

   b. 256 MB

   c. 448 MB

   d. 64 MB

7. Susan calls from an off-site location telling you that she cannot connect to the wireless hot spot using her laptop. When she opens the Wireless Network Connections window, she sees the message, "No wireless networks were found in range," although she knows that others around her are wirelessly connected. What do you tell Susan to do? Choose the *two* best answers.

   a. Right-click the Wireless Network Connection window and choose Repair from the shortcut menu.

   b. Verify that the wireless switch near the hinge of her laptop is turned on.

   c. Verify the LCD panel of her laptop is fully raised.

   d. Step Susan through the process of reinstalling her wireless adapter's drivers.

   e. Reboot the laptop.

8. How can you tell that a laptop battery is fully charged?

   a. Check the icon in the system tray, which should indicate a full charge.

   b. The battery light on the front of the laptop is red.

   c. The battery icon in the system tray is green.

   d. Double-click the Power Options icon in Control Panel and select the Advanced tab.

9. When a laptop connected to a network goes into hibernation, which of the following statements is true?
   a. The laptop is in ACPI S3 mode.
   b. Everything in RAM has been copied to the hard drive and the system is shut down.
   c. The hard drive, monitor, and processor are turned off, but RAM is still active.
   d. The only way to start up the system is to press the power button.
10. Tom is a traveling salesman who uses his laptop extensively while making customer calls. His laptop battery loses its charge before the day is done. Which of the following solutions will best help Tom?
   a. Purchase a second battery pack for his laptop.
   b. Purchase a 20 volt DC power adapter to power the laptop from his car.
   c. Calibrate his laptop to consume less power.
   d. Replace his battery pack for one with a higher voltage rating.
11. Which of the following is the fastest wireless standard?
   a. Bluetooth
   b. 802.11b
   c. 802.11g
   d. Ethernet
12. A user complains that the trackpad on his laptop does not work. What is a possible cause of the problem?
   a. The user has connected an external PS/2 mouse to the laptop.
   b. The user is trying to use a stylus to work the trackpad rather than his fingers.
   c. The trackpad switch at the top of the laptop is turned off.
   d. The application the user has open does not recognize a trackpad.
13. Janice wants to use an external monitor with her laptop. She has connected the monitor and used the Fn key to direct output to both the LCD panel and the monitor. Both displays are the same. How does Janice configure her laptop so that she can open one application window on the LCD panel and another on the external monitor?
   a. Use the Fn key with a function key to toggle the display a second time.
   b. Use the Settings tab of the Display Properties window to extend the Windows desktop to the second monitor.
   c. Use the Dual Monitor icon in Control Panel to configure the second monitor.
   d. In Windows, install a second set of video drivers for the external monitor.

14. Jack's laptop has been dropped and he brings it to you for repair. When you turn on the laptop, it does not receive any power—you see no lights and you don't hear the fans. When you try a different AC adapter, the laptop still has no power. Jack tells you his first priority is to recover the important data on the laptop. What is your next step?

    a. Tell Jack the data cannot be recovered unless he is willing to pay an expensive data recovery service to do the job.

    b. Replace the internal power supply.

    c. Remove the hard drive from the laptop and use an IDE-to-USB adapter to connect the hard drive to a desktop computer.

    d. Replace the motherboard.

15. A laptop has one Type III PCMCIA slot, and the user has upgraded the OS on the laptop from Windows 98 to Windows XP. Which of the following statements is true?

    a. You can install one Type I card and one Type II card in the single Type III slot.

    b. You can install one ExpressCard/34 card in the Type III slot.

    c. Because Windows XP does not support the outdated Type III PCMCIA slots, the laptop can no longer use this slot.

    d. You can install one PC Card in the Type III slot.

CHAPTER 3

Operating Systems

Troubleshooting scenarios in this chapter:

- **Scenario 3.1:** Clean Up Startup
- **Scenario 3.2:** Troubleshoot a Startup Problem
- **Scenario 3.3:** Troubleshoot Windows Installations

SUMMARY OF DOMAIN CONTENT

This section of the chapter contains a summary overview of the content in the CompTIA A+ 220-602 Domain 3, *Operating Systems*, and 220-603 Domain 2, *Operating Systems*. Please note that the A+ 220-604 exam does not include the *Operating Systems* domain. Also, CompTIA includes the following statement to make it clear about which operating systems are tested:

Unless otherwise noted, operating systems referred to in these objectives include Microsoft Windows 2000, Windows XP Professional, Windows XP Home and Windows XP Media Center.

The high-level objectives for this domain are:

- Identify the fundamental principles of operating systems
- Install, configure, optimize and upgrade operating systems—references to upgrading from Windows 95 and NT may be made
- Identify tools, diagnostic procedures and troubleshooting techniques for operating systems
- Perform preventive maintenance for operating systems

IDENTIFY THE FUNDAMENTAL PRINCIPLES OF OPERATING SYSTEMS

***Use command-line functions and utilities to manage operating systems, including proper syntax and switches for example*:**

- *CMD*
  Using the command **Cmd** or **Cmd.exe** in the Run dialog box opens a command prompt window. In this window, you can use wildcard characters in filenames. When working in this window, type **Ctrl+C** to break a running program. To exit the window, type **exit** and press **Enter**.
- *HELP*
  Provides help about any command. Alternately, you can use the /? parameter at the end of a specific command such as in DIR /?.
- *DIR*
  Lists files and directories.
- *ATTRIB*
  Displays and changes the read-only, archive, system, and hidden attributes assigned to files.
- *EDIT*
  Edit is a text editor you can use to create or edit a batch file or other text file.
- *COPY*
  Copies a file or group of files. The original file is not altered.
- *XCOPY*
  More powerful than the Copy command, Xcopy can copy files, directories, and subdirectories. Use parameters to enhance its functions.
- *FORMAT*
  Formats partitions on hard drives, and formats floppy disks.
- *IPCONFIG*
  Displays TCP/IP configuration information (IPCONFIG/ALL) and releases (IPCONFIG/RELEASE) and renews (IPCONFIG/RENEW) IP addresses. In Windows XP, you can also release and renew an IP address using the Repair command from the Network Connections window.

- *PING*
  Tests a network connection by asking another host on the network to respond.
- *MD/CD/RD*
  MD (Make Directory) creates a directory. CD (Change Directory) changes the default directory. RD (Remove Directory) deletes a directory and all its contents.

Identify concepts and procedures for creating, viewing and managing disks, directories and files on operating systems

- *Disks (e.g., active, primary, extended and logical partitions and file systems including FAT32 and NTFS)*
  - The active partition contains and boots the OS. Windows 2000/XP calls the active partition the system partition. A primary partition is a partition on a hard drive that can contain only one logical drive or volume. An extended partition can contain more than one logical drive. A logical partition, also called a logical drive or volume, is a portion or all of a partition that is treated as a drive by the OS, such as drive C or drive E.
  - FAT32 and NTFS are the two file systems supported by Windows 2000/XP. Use NTFS for better security and drive management. For example, folder and file encryption and disk quotas are available when using NTFS, but not available when using FAT32.
  - The Mac OS X operating system by Apple Computers is based on a UNIX core and can read (not write to) NTFS drives.
- *Directory structures (e.g., create folders, navigate directory structures)*
  Use Windows Explorer to view and manage the directory structure.
- *Files (e.g., creation, attributes, permissions)*
  Use Windows Explorer or the Attrib command to manage file attributes. File permissions are granted to user accounts and groups of accounts to control security and meet the job requirements of each user. Know how to assign file permissions so that some users on a network can access a file but others can't. Use the Computer Management console to create and manage user accounts and user groups. Disable simple file sharing so that you can control which user or group has access to a file or folder.

Locate and use operating system utilities and available switches for example:

- *Disk management tools (e.g., DEFRAG, NTBACKUP, CHKDSK, Format)*
  - Defrag is used to rearrange clusters of files in contiguous chains.
  - Ntbackup is the Windows 2000/XP backup utility used to back up the entire hard drive, data, or the system state.
  - Use Chkdsk with parameters to fix file system errors and recover data from bad sectors; Chkdsk does not actually repair a bad sector. To check drive C for file system errors and repair them, use the command CHKDSK C: /F. To repair file system errors on drive C and also attempt to recover data from bad sectors, use the command CHKDSK C: /R.
- *System management tools*
  - *Device and Task Manager*
    Device Manager is the primary tool to manage hardware, troubleshoot problems with hardware, update device drivers, and uninstall devices. Task Manager can

manage running applications, display and end processes, and display information about CPU performance, network performance, and logged-on users.

- *MSCONFIG.EXE*
  Msconfig.exe displays services and other programs that are launched at startup. Use it to temporarily disable a startup program while troubleshooting a startup problem.
- *REGEDIT.EXE*
  Regedit.exe is the one Windows XP registry editor. Windows 2000 offers two registry editors: Regedit and Regedt32. Windows 2000 Regedit lets you export keys, and Windows 2000 Regedt32 lets you work in read-only mode.
- *REGEDT32.EXE*
  One of two Windows 2000 registry editors. In Windows XP, if you use the Regedt32 command, the Regedit editor is launched.
- *CMD*
  CMD opens a command prompt window.
- *Event Viewer*
  Event Viewer is an MMC snap-in that maintains a list of hardware, application, system, and security events. Use it when troubleshooting to search for logged error events such as a failure to write to the hard drive. It can also be used to monitor and log security events such as a failed attempt to log onto the system. Note this last feature is not available under Windows XP Home.
- *System Restore*
  This Windows XP utility maintains a group of restore points that can be used to restore critical system files to a previous state. You can restore the system using System Restore from the Windows desktop or when using Safe Mode. During startup, if Windows recognizes a problem, it offers to restore the system before launching the desktop.
- *Remote Desktop*
  This tool allows you to operate your Windows XP desktop from anywhere on the Internet.
- *File management tools (e.g., Windows Explorer, ATTRIB.EXE)*
  Windows Explorer is the primary tool for file management. Use Attrib from a command prompt window to display and change file attributes.

INSTALL, CONFIGURE, OPTIMIZE AND UPGRADE OPERATING SYSTEMS—REFERENCES TO UPGRADING FROM WINDOWS 95 AND NT MAY BE MADE

Be aware of these allowed upgrade paths:

- Windows 98, Windows Me, Windows NT 4.0, or Windows 2000 can be upgraded to Windows XP Professional.
- Windows 98 or Windows Me can be upgraded to Windows XP Home Edition.
- You cannot upgrade Windows 95 to Windows XP Home Edition or Windows XP Professional.
- All versions of Windows 95/98/Me and Windows NT Workstation 3.51 and higher can be upgraded to Windows 2000.

Identify procedures and utilities used to optimize operating systems for example:

- ***Virtual memory***
  Virtual memory is stored in the swap file, Pagefile.sys, on the hard drive, normally in the root of drive C. Change virtual memory settings from the Performance Options dialog box, which is accessed using the Advanced tab on the System Properties dialog box.
- ***Hard drives (e.g., disk defragmentation)***
  Clean up the hard drive, delete temporary files, and defrag the hard drive at least monthly.
- ***Temporary files***
  Delete temporary files using the drive Properties window.
- ***Services***
  Services are managed using the Services console, Services.msc.
- ***Startup***
  Msconfig can be used to troubleshoot startup processes. Other tools to manage startup are the Services console, Add or Remove Programs applet in Control Panel, startup folders, Task Scheduler, and Group Policy.
- ***Application***
  Applications are managed using the Add or Remove Programs applet in Control Panel.

IDENTIFY TOOLS, DIAGNOSTIC PROCEDURES AND TROUBLESHOOTING TECHNIQUES FOR OPERATING SYSTEMS

Demonstrate the ability to recover operating systems (e.g., boot methods, recovery console, ASR, ERD) (220-602 only)

Boot methods to use when troubleshooting are the Advanced Options Menu (accessed by pressing F8 at startup and shown in Figure 3-1), Last Known Good Configuration, Safe Mode, and the Recovery Console. If the Windows installation is corrupted, use the Windows XP Automated System Recovery (ASR) to restore the system to the last ASR backup. For Windows 2000, use the Emergency Repair Disk (ERD) to return Windows to its state when first installed.

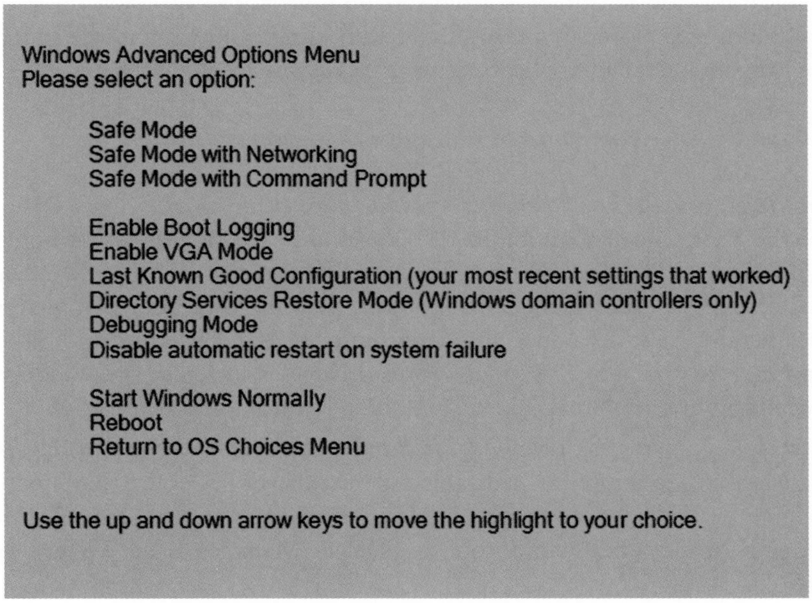

```
Windows Advanced Options Menu
Please select an option:

    Safe Mode
    Safe Mode with Networking
    Safe Mode with Command Prompt

    Enable Boot Logging
    Enable VGA Mode
    Last Known Good Configuration (your most recent settings that worked)
    Directory Services Restore Mode (Windows domain controllers only)
    Debugging Mode
    Disable automatic restart on system failure

    Start Windows Normally
    Reboot
    Return to OS Choices Menu

Use the up and down arrow keys to move the highlight to your choice.
```

Figure 3-1 Press the F8 key at startup to display the Windows XP Advanced Options Menu

Recognize and resolve common operational problems for example:

- ***Windows specific printing problems (e.g., print spool stalled, incorrect/incompatible driver form print)***
  Use the Windows XP Printers and Faxes window or the Windows 2000 Printers window to cancel print jobs, clear the print spool, update printer drivers, and install and enable additional printer components.
- ***Auto-restart errors***
  In Windows XP, on the Advanced Options Menu, choose "Disable automatic restart on system failure" to prevent a stop error from rebooting the system, which can cause Windows to endlessly recycle startup. To modify this setting from the Windows desktop, use the Advanced tab on the System Properties window.
- ***Bluescreen error***
  A blue screen error, also called a stop error or Blue screen of death (BSOD), displays a 10-numeral hex number that indicates the cause of the error, and causes the system to halt or to reboot. If you can boot into Safe Mode, search Event Viewer for clues. Also, search for the 10-numeral hex number on the Microsoft Web site for information about the error.
- ***System lock-up***
  Use Task Manager to end a process that is not responding. Search Event Viewer for logged errors to help find the source of the problem. Use the System Properties window or System Information (Msinfo32.exe) to verify you have enough memory for Windows to function and view hardware and diagnostic information.
- ***Device drivers failure (input/output devices)***
  Device drivers are managed, viewed, and updated using Device Manager. The Services console can show if a driver is to be loaded at startup. Use Enable VGA mode on the Advanced Options Menu to use a generic video driver. Use Enable Boot Logging on the Advanced Options Menu to find the name of a driver that failed during startup. The Sigverif.exe program can verify that drivers are digitally signed.
- ***Application install, start or load failure***
  Applications are managed from the Add or Remove Programs applet in Control Panel. Applications can be launched from startup folders, the Task Scheduler, the Start menu, or Windows Explorer. Windows Error Reporting can help find the source of an error. You can end a stalled application using Task Manager.

Recognize and resolve common error messages and codes for example:

- ***Boot (e.g., invalid boot disk, inaccessible boot drive, missing NTLDR)***
  Use the boot sequence option in CMOS setup to set the priority of boot devices. NTLDR is the Windows boot loader stored in the root of drive C. Other files in the root directory needed to boot are Boot.ini (text file with boot parameters), Bootsect.dos (used in a dual boot environment), Ntdetect.com, and Ntbootdd.sys (optional; used in a SCSI system). Some other files stored in the Windows folder needed to boot are Ntoskrnl.exe, Hal.dll, and Ntdll.dll.
- ***Startup (e.g., device/service has failed to start, device/program in registry not found)***
  Use Msconfig to temporarily disable a device driver or service. Use Enable Boot Logging on the Advanced Options Menu to find the name of a service that failed during startup. Other helpful tools are Device Manager, Event Viewer, and the Services console.

- *Event Viewer*
  Search it for logged errors at startup or when applications or hardware fail.
- *Registry*
  Services, drivers, and applications can be loaded from the registry. Before editing the registry, export the key you will be editing so you can backtrack if necessary. The Export command is on the File menu of the registry editor.
- *Windows reporting*
  Windows Error Reporting displays links to the Microsoft Web site for suggestions when solving applications and Windows errors.

Use diagnostic utilities and tools to resolve operational problems for example:

- *Bootable media*
  Boot from the Windows setup CD to load the Recovery Console or repair a Windows installation. Some computer, hard drive, and notebook manufacturers offer diagnostic utilities on bootable CDs. Boot from these CDs to test hardware for errors.
- *Startup modes (e.g., safe mode, safe mode with command prompt or networking, step-by-step/single step mode)*
  The Windows XP Advanced Options Menu offers Safe Mode (loads the Windows desktop), Safe Mode with command prompt (use commands to troubleshoot), and Safe Mode with networking (network access to download fixes or access a network server). Single step startup mode is not available using Windows 2000/XP.
- *Documentation resources (e.g., user/installation manuals, internet/web based, training materials)*
  Organizations that PC support technicians work for have training manuals for their technicians. You also need available user manuals for all applications you support, which might be available on software manufacturers' Web sites. The Web is your most useful source for documentation. Look on hardware manufacturers' Web sites for service manuals, user documentation, and FAQs.
- *Task and Device Manager*
  Use Task Manager to end an unresponsive task. Use Device Manager to troubleshoot hardware problems.
- *Event Viewer*
  For hardware, applications, security, performance, and startup errors, search Event Viewer logs.
- *MSCONFIG*
  Use the System Configuration Utility (Msconfig.exe) to view contents of Boot.ini and services and startup processes. You can also temporarily disable a startup program when troubleshooting startup.
- *Recovery CD/Recovery partition*
  A brand name PC or notebook is likely to have a hidden recovery partition on the hard drive that contains diagnostic software and programs and files to rebuild the Windows installation. This same software might be available on recovery CDs. For a notebook computer or brand name PC, use these tools to reinstall Windows rather than using a regular Windows setup CD.
- *Remote Desktop Connection and Assistance*
  Use Windows XP Remote Assistance to help a novice user from a remote computer on a local network or over the Internet. Firewalls that sit between you and the computer

and user that you are trying to help might pose a problem. Use Remote Desktop to control a Windows XP computer from anywhere on the Internet.

- *System File Checker (SFC)*
  Use SFC from a command prompt window on the Windows 2000/XP desktop to verify and refresh versions of system files.

PERFORM PREVENTIVE MAINTENANCE FOR OPERATING SYSTEMS

Demonstrate the ability to perform preventive maintenance on operating systems including software and Windows updates (e.g., service packs), scheduled backups/restore, restore points

Windows XP has Automatic Updates, which can be configured from the Automatic Updates tab on the System Properties dialog box. Best practice is to allow it to work in the background to keep Windows updated. Manually apply updates at least monthly on every computer you support. Major updates are called service packs. Schedule backups when users are not busy, such as in the middle of the night. Set a Windows XP restore point before making changes to the system. Know that when you return the system to a restore point, you might lose a new user account you have created after the restore point was made. You will not lose the user's data files.

SCENARIO 3.1: CLEAN UP STARTUP

OBJECTIVES

The goal of this lab is to help you learn how to clean up a slow Windows XP startup process that might display errors. After completing this lab, you will be able to:

- Use Windows tools to clean up startup.
- Investigate processes that are slowing down Windows.
- Configure the system to keep it clean and free of malware.

MATERIALS REQUIRED

This lab requires the following:

- A Windows XP computer designated for this lab
- Internet access

LAB PREPARATION

Before lab begins, the instructor or lab assistant needs to do the following:

- Make available a Windows XP computer. For the best student experience, try to use systems that are not optimized and need the benefits of this lab.
- Verify that Internet access is available.

SCENARIO BACKGROUND

A troubleshooting problem you'll often face as a PC support technician is a sluggish Windows system. Customers might tell you that when their Windows XP computer was new, it ran smoothly and fast with no errors, but now it hangs occasionally, is slow to start up or shut down, and is slow when working. There is no one particular problem that stands out above the rest, but a customer just says, "Please make my system work faster." When solving these types of general problems, it helps to have a game plan. This activity will give you just that. You'll learn how to speed up Windows, ridding it of unneeded and unwanted processes that are slowing it down. After you have completed cleaning up Windows, if the system is still slow, it's time to look at possible hardware upgrades to improve performance. How to do that was covered in Chapter 1. Also, if you encounter error messages during startup or the system refuses to boot, know that troubleshooting startup errors is covered in the next lab.

ESTIMATED COMPLETION TIME: 1.5 hours

SCENARIO

Before you make any changes to the system, first get a benchmark of how long it takes for Windows to start up. Do the following:

1. Power down the computer and turn it on. Using a watch with a second hand, note how many minutes are needed for the system to start. Startup is completed after you have logged onto Windows XP and the hourglass has disappeared and the hard drive activity light has stopped. How long does startup take?

   ____

2. Describe any problems you observed during startup.

   ____

   ____

This lab assumes that Windows might be slow starting, but does start up without errors. If you see error messages on screen or the system refuses to boot, you need to solve these problems before you continue with a general cleanup. To solve startup problems, first complete Scenario 3.2, Troubleshoot a Startup Problem, and then return to this lab.

TROUBLESHOOTING

You're now ready to begin a general cleanup. Do the following:

1. In a work environment, ask the user if valuable data is on the hard drive that is not backed up. If so, back up that data now.
2. Run antivirus (AV) software. Here are your options:
   - If AV software is not installed and you have the AV software setup CD, install it. If it fails to install (some viruses block software installations), boot into Safe Mode and install and run it from there.
   - If you don't have access to the AV software setup CD, you can download software from the Internet. If your PC cannot connect to the Internet (such as when Internet access is blocked by an active virus), you can download the software on another PC and burn a CD with the downloaded file. But before you do that, first try to connect to the Internet using the Safe Mode with Networking option on the Advanced Options Menu. (This option might not load a virus that prevents Internet access.)

- If you don't have AV software installed and don't have access to an AV software setup CD, but you can connect the computer to the Internet, you can run an online virus scan from an AV Web site. For example, TrendMicro (*www.trendmicro.com*) offers a free online virus scan. (This free online scan has been known to find viruses that other scans do not.)
- List the steps you took to run the AV software:

- List any malware the AV software found:

3. Reboot the system. Is there a performance increase? How long does startup take?

4. If the system is still running so slowly you find it difficult to work, you can temporarily use Msconfig to control startup processes hogging system resources. Enter **Msconfig** in the Run dialog box and press **Enter**, which opens the System Configuration Utility window. Click the **Services** tab (see Figure 3-2). Check **Hide All Microsoft Services.** You can keep other services from starting by unchecking them in this window. On the Startup tab, you can uncheck other startup processes you want to prevent from launching at startup. Reboot the system to cause these changes to take effect.

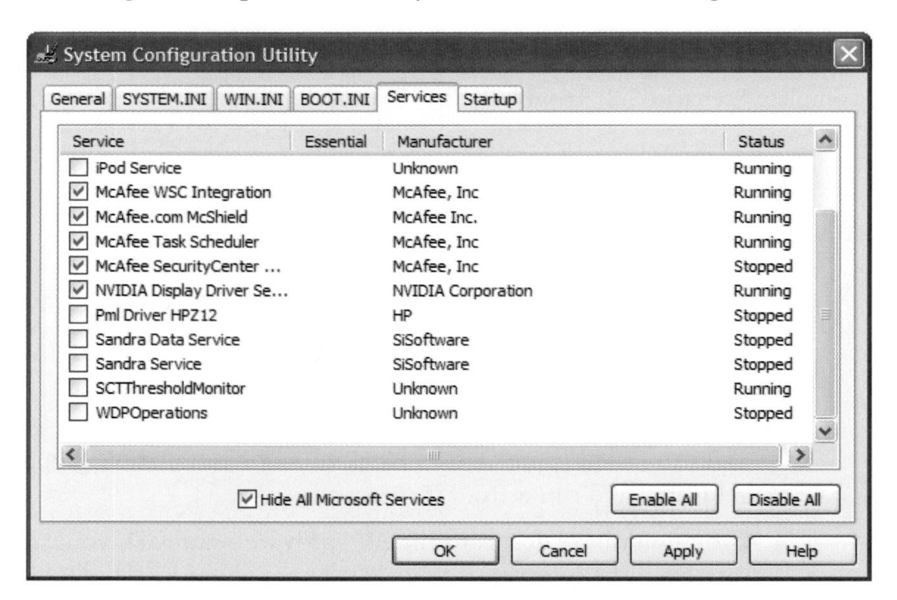

Figure 3-2 Use the System Configuration Utility window to control startup processes until you can further clean up a slow Windows system

If you suspect the system is still infected, such as when your browser shows uninvited pop-up windows, you might still have malware. Try installing and running Windows Defender by Microsoft (*www.microsoft.com*) or Ad-Aware by Lavasoft (*www.lavasoft.com*).

5. Use the Add or Remove Programs applet in Control Panel to uninstall any unwanted software. What software did you find that needed to be uninstalled?

____

6. Reboot the system. Is there a performance increase? How long does startup take?

____

7. Clean up the hard drive. Delete temporary files, defrag the hard drive, and check for errors. If the system is slow while doing these tasks, do them from Safe Mode. Note that you need about 15 percent free hard drive space to defragment the drive. If you don't have that much free space, find some folders and files you can move to a different media. Windows requires this much free space to run well.
8. Reboot the system. Is there a performance increase? How long does startup take?

____

The next step is to search for programs, services, and other processes launched at startup that can be removed from the startup process. The following startup folders can contain programs or shortcuts:

- C:\Documents and Settings*CurrentUser*\Start Menu\Programs\Startup
- C:\Documents and Settings\All Users\Start Menu\Programs\Startup
- C:\Windows\Profiles\All Users\Start Menu\Programs\Startup
- C:\Windows\Profiles*CurrentUser*\Start Menu\Programs\Startup

Scripts used by Group Policy can be stored in these folders:

- C:\WINDOWS\System32\GroupPolicy\Machine\Scripts\Startup
- C:\WINDOWS\System32\GroupPolicy\Machine\Scripts\Shutdown
- C:\WINDOWS\System32\GroupPolicy\User\Scripts\Logon
- C:\WINDOWS\System32\GroupPolicy\User\Scripts\Logoff

Scheduled tasks are stored in this folder:

- C:\Windows\Tasks

9. Check all the nine folders listed above for shortcuts or programs. If you are not sure an item belongs in the folder, move it to another folder and restart the system to test for errors. What items did you find and where did you put them?

____

____

____

10. Check Device Manager for hardware devices that are installed but not working or devices that are no longer needed and should be uninstalled. Did you find any devices that need fixing or uninstalling? How did you handle the situation?

____

____

11. Windows loads all installed fonts at startup. Doing so does not normally slow down a system unless too many fonts are installed. Check the C:\Windows\Fonts folder. If you find more than 260 entries in this folder, extra fonts have been installed. Try moving some to another folder. Then reboot twice. The first reboot rebuilds the fonts list, so it will take the second reboot before you see performance improvement.

12. Reboot the system. How long does startup take?

____

If Windows is still slow to load, you need to dig deeper into startup processes. Just after a restart, open Task Manager. Investigate all processes that are not part of normal Windows operations. Figure 3-3 can help you as it lists the bare-bones Windows XP startup processes immediately after a fresh Windows installation.

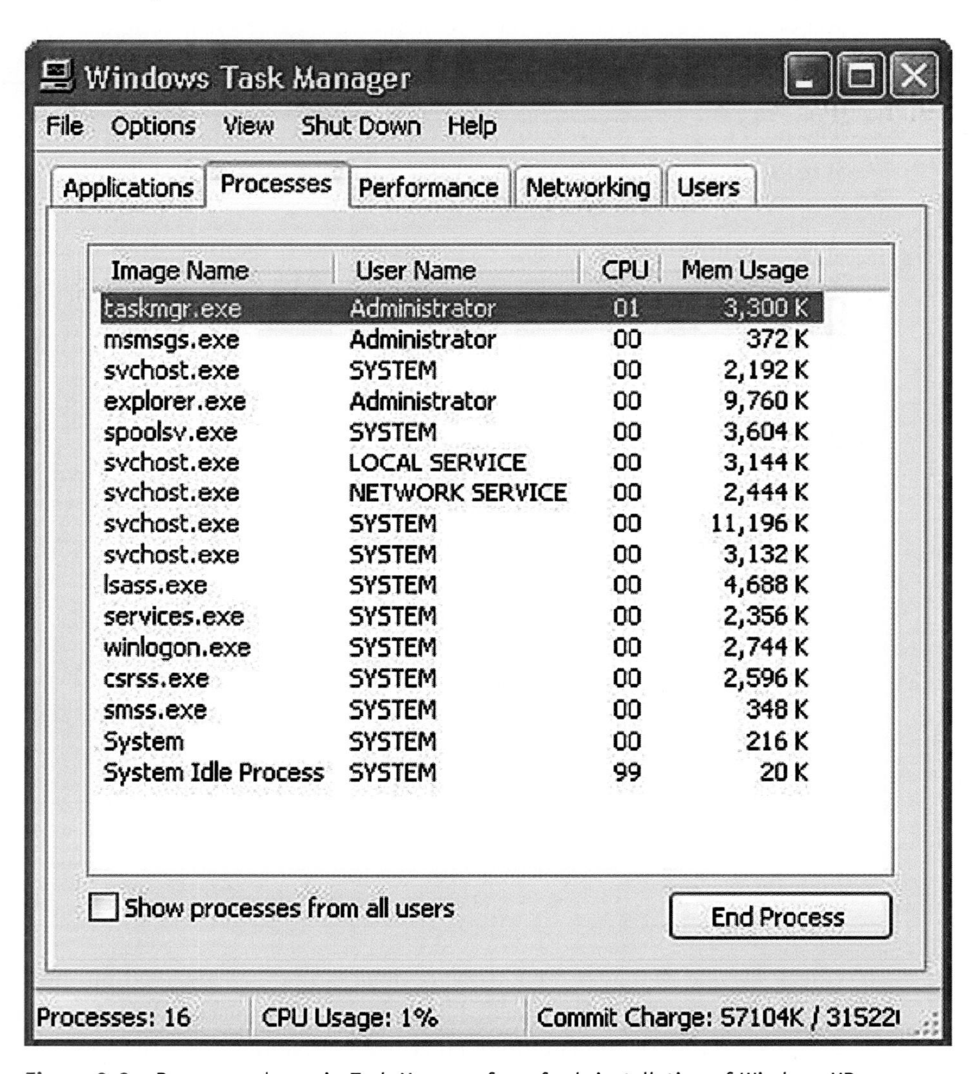

Figure 3-3 Processes shown in Task Manager for a fresh installation of Windows XP

1. List all the nonessential processes running on your system with a short description of the purpose of each process. For unknown processes, try searching the Internet for information.

____

____

2. Of the processes listed above, should any be removed from startup? List the process and how you removed it.

3. Reboot the system. How long does startup take?

Now that you have the system cleaned, you want to keep it that way. Do the following:

1. Install and configure the AV software to launch every time Windows is started. Instruct the user on how to keep the software up to date and renew the annual license for the software.
2. Set the Windows XP Firewall to stop uninvited activity from the network.
3. Configure Windows XP to automatically download and apply updates.

REVIEW QUESTIONS

1. If AV software is not installed and you don't have access to the Internet, how can you install it?

2. Which utility is used to uninstall applications?

3. Which window is used to defrag a hard drive and check it for errors?

4. What two folders can contain programs to be launched when a specific user logs onto the system?

5. When cleaning up startup, why should you not delete a program file you find in a startup folder?

6. What utility lists all currently running processes?

7. After you have done all you can to speed up startup and Windows operations, if the system is still sluggish, which hardware device should you check first for a possible bottleneck?

SCENARIO 3.2: TROUBLESHOOT A STARTUP PROBLEM

OBJECTIVES

The goal of this lab is to help you learn how to troubleshoot a problem that occurs during Windows XP startup. After completing this lab, you will be able to:

- Solve startup problems with Windows XP.
- Use Windows tools to recover data when Windows will not boot.

MATERIALS REQUIRED

This lab requires the following:

- A Windows XP computer designated for this lab
- Files on the Windows XP setup CD
- Internet access

LAB PREPARATION

Before the lab begins, the instructor or lab assistant needs to do the following:

- Verify a Windows XP computer is working for each student or workgroup.
- Make available the Windows XP setup CD or setup files stored on the network or other location.
- Verify that Internet access is available.

SCENARIO BACKGROUND

As stable as Windows XP is, problems can still occur. A PC support technician needs to know how to investigate these problems and solve them. This lab gives you a variety of experiences to help build your troubleshooting skills.

ESTIMATED COMPLETION TIME: 2 hours

SCENARIO

Karen calls you in a desperate voice and says, "Please come over to my desk right away. My PC has crashed and I have an important Word document on it that isn't backed up. I have to have it for a closing tomorrow morning." As the only PC support technician in a small real estate firm, you find yourself responding far too often to desperate cries for help, and you've learned that protecting user data is actually the most important part of your job. For that reason, you have just installed a file backup server for the company. However, it's up to each user to decide to use the server. Therefore, you're a bit frustrated when you arrive at Karen's desk. Why didn't she back up like everyone else in her group is now doing?

TROUBLESHOOTING

Karen steps aside for you to take over the problem. On the black screen, you see a simple text message, "Invalid boot disk." You try not to alarm Karen as you suck in your breath with a soft whistle. Answer these questions:

1. What do you do next?

____

2. After you power down the system and turn it back on, you get the same message. Next, you try booting from the Windows XP setup CD. You get the same message. What do you do now?

____

____

3. On the next boot, you are able to launch the Windows XP Recovery Console. Karen says the Word document is in her My Documents folder and is named MichaelSmithClosing.doc. What is the exact path to the document? (Karen's user account is Karen Moore.)

____

4. Create an account named Karen Moore on your lab PC and put a file named MichaelSmithClosing.doc in the My Documents folder for this account.
5. List the commands to copy the document to a floppy disk in drive A, and test these commands at your lab PC using the Recovery Console.

____

____

____

____

____

____

____

____

6. When you try to access drive C on Karen's PC, you receive an error message, "The path or file specified is not valid." You suspect a damaged master boot record. (More accurately, you *hope* the problem is this simple to solve!) What command can you use to fix this MBR?

____

7. What command can you use to check the hard drive for errors and possibly recover lost data?

____

If this last command works, then you can most likely recover Karen's file. You should not trust this hard drive again. In a work environment, you should copy all data to another media, replace the drive, and reinstall Windows XP.

1. If you were not able to recover Karen's file, what can you tactfully say to Karen about the lost file and the need to make backups in the future?

____

____

2. Assume you were able to recover the file. After the file is safely in Karen's hands, what can you say to her to encourage her to use backups in the future?

____

____

Sometimes problems are not the result of failed hardware, but are caused by corrupted device drivers. If an error message appears during the boot that names the device or driver causing the problem, you can try to disable the device. If the error message goes away, reinstall the device or update the device drivers. Sometimes the error message doesn't contain enough information or there is no error message at all—the boot just hangs. Complete the following steps to learn how to handle these situations:

1. Boot to the Advanced Options Menu and enable boot logging. What is the path and name of the boot log file?

____

2. Now reboot with boot logging enabled. The system hangs, but hopefully the log contains enough information to help you solve the problem.
3. Boot into Safe Mode and view the log file. How do you display the log file on screen?

____

If you have a copy of a boot log file created when the system was healthy, you can compare the problem log file to the healthy one to help locate the source of the problem. Do the following:

1. On your lab PC, enable boot logging and reboot the system.
2. Open a command prompt window. List the commands to copy the log file to a floppy disk.

____

____

____

Tools and utilities that can help you solve Windows problems are listed below:

- Last Known Good Configuration on the Advanced Options Menu
- Safe Mode on the Advanced Options Menu
- Boot logging on the Advanced Options Menu
- Antivirus software
- Device Manager
- System Configuration Utility (Msconfig)
- System Restore
- Task Manager
- Services console
- Add or Remove Programs applet in Control Panel
- Drive Properties window (Defrag, disk cleanup, error correcting)

Using the preceding list and other resources, answer the following questions:

1. What tool can be used to view all services loaded at startup or loaded as needed?

 ____

2. What tool can be used to view all installed devices and their drivers?

 ____

3. What tool can be used to view write errors to the hard drive?

 ____

4. What tool can be used to view running processes?

 ____

5. If you cannot boot to the normal Windows desktop, but you can boot into Safe Mode, which tool can you use to systematically identify the service or driver causing the problem?

 ____

6. What function key is used to access the Advanced Options Menu?

 ____

7. What function key is used to boot directly into Safe Mode?

 ____

REVIEW QUESTIONS

1. You have just installed new software and restarted the system, which now hangs before reaching the Windows desktop. What do you try first?

 ____

2. The system hangs while Windows XP is loading, but no error message displays. How can you determine which driver, program, or service is the source of the error?

 ____

3. After you have logged into Windows XP, a strange error message appears about a service that failed to load. How can you find out from where this service is launched?

 ____

4. Users complain that data files are getting corrupted and you suspect the hard drive might be failing. What utility can you use to view problems recorded when writing to the drive?

 ____

5. Numerous error messages appear as you load Windows, and you suspect the system is infected with a virus. No antivirus software is installed, but when you try to install the software from CD, you get error messages. What do you do next?

 ____

SCENARIO 3.3: TROUBLESHOOT WINDOWS INSTALLATIONS

OBJECTIVES

The goal of this lab is to help you learn how to troubleshoot problems with installing Windows XP. After completing this lab, you will be able to:

- Research problems with Windows installations and moving user data and preferences.
- Understand how to do an unattended installation.

MATERIALS REQUIRED

This lab requires the following:

- A Windows XP computer designated for this lab
- Internet access

LAB PREPARATION

Before the lab begins, the instructor or lab assistant needs to do the following:

- Verify that Internet access is available.

SCENARIO BACKGROUND

PC support technicians are often called on to upgrade Windows or install Windows on a new hard drive. Installations don't always go smoothly, so you need to know what to do when problems arise. When researching a problem, the Microsoft support site (*support.microsoft.com*) is an excellent resource. To save time and assure that standards are followed, large organizations often deploy Windows using unattended installations. Even though you might not be responsible for developing the procedures to perform unattended installations, you still need to know about them so you can assist as needed. You also need to know about transferring user settings and data from one computer to another. All these skills are covered in this lab.

ESTIMATED COMPLETION TIME: 45 minutes

SCENARIOS AND TROUBLESHOOTING

As a PC support technician in a large organization, you work on a team of ten technicians supporting the users and equipment on a large enterprise network including personal computers, laptops, printers, and scanners. Corporations are sometimes slow to upgrade operating systems and equipment, and several users in the organization use Mac computers, so you find yourself researching many problems as they arise. Research these problems and answer the following questions:

1. A group of PCs are being converted from Windows 2000 to Windows XP, and your coworker, Larry, has set up these unattended installations of Windows XP using the System Preparation (Sysprep) utility. Larry is not available and your boss has asked you to make a change to the answer file on a particular desktop computer. He gives you the change he wants you to make but assumes you know the name of the answer file and its location on the computer that is about to have Windows XP installed.

- What is the name of the answer file for the unattended Windows installation?

  ____

- You know that Windows will be installed in the C:\Windows folder. What is the path to the answer file?

  ____

2. You are asked to enable disk quotas on a Windows XP computer that serves double duty as a user's PC and a file server. When you begin to make the change, you notice that the Properties window for the drive used as the file server (drive D) does not have the Quota tab.

   - What would cause the Quota tab to be missing?

     ____

   - What command can you use from a command prompt window to convert the FAT32 drive D to a NTFS drive?

     ____

3. Linda has just received a new desktop computer on which Windows XP has been newly installed. Her old Windows XP computer and her new computer are both connected to the network. After you move data and user preferences to the new computer, you intend to reformat the old computer's hard drive, reinstall Windows XP and applications, and assign the computer to another user.

   - What are two Windows XP utilities that can be used to transfer Linda's My Documents folder and user preferences from her old Windows XP computer to this new computer?

     ____

     ____

   - Which of these two tools is best to use in this situation? Why?

     ____

   - Your company policy is to keep the old computer in your storage room for one month before reformatting the hard drive. Why do you think this policy is needed?

     ____

4. Jennifer is a graphics artist who works a lot with Adobe Illustrator on her desktop PC, but occasionally works at a customer's location where she uses the same application on a Mac. She wants to use a FireWire external hard drive with her desktop PC at work that she can take with her to the off-site location and have the Mac read her large files on the external drive. Answer these questions:

   - If she uses the NTFS file system on the external drive, can files be read by the Mac?

     ____

   - Can files be written to the drive by the Mac?

     ____

   - Can the Mac execute software that has been installed by the PC on the external drive?

     ____

REVIEW QUESTIONS

1. What file system is required if you are using disk quotas?

___

2. What file system is the default file system for Mac OS X?

___

3. From which server operating system was the Mac OS X operating system by Apple Computers derived?

___

4. What is the name and path to the answer file for an unattended installation on drive D that has been prepared by SysPrep?

___

PRACTICE EXAM

The following practice exam covers the domain, *Operating Systems*. Answers to the odd-numbered questions are provided in Appendix B.

1. When you try to restart a Windows XP system, errors about corrupted system files appear and the normal Windows desktop refuses to load. The user tells you there is important data on the hard drive that is not backed up. What do you try next?
   - a. Start up the Windows desktop in Safe Mode and then copy the data to another media.
   - b. Use the System Restore utility on the Windows XP setup CD to repair the system files, and then back up the data.
   - c. Use the ASR process to repair the Windows installation and then back up the data.
   - d. Use the Recovery Console to start the system and copy the data to another media.
2. How do you launch the Windows XP ASR utility to recover a Windows installation?
   - a. Choose ASR Recovery from the Start, All Programs menu.
   - b. Choose Automated System Recovery from the Windows XP Advanced Options Menu.
   - c. Press F2 after booting from the Windows XP setup CD.
   - d. Boot from the ASR disc that you made when you first installed Windows XP.
3. When will using a Windows 2000 ERD not be able to recover a Windows 2000 installation?
   - a. When the user has data on the hard drive that is not backed up.
   - b. When the Windows System Root folder is corrupted or missing.
   - c. When you cannot launch the Recovery Console.
   - d. When the System State has not been backed up.
4. When repairing a Windows XP installation, which order of fixes is appropriate to use?
   - a. ASR, ERD, Safe Mode, System Restore, reinstall Windows XP.
   - b. Reinstall Windows XP, System Restore, Safe Mode, Recovery Console.

c. System Restore, Safe Mode, Recovery Console, ASR, System File Check

d. Last Known Good Configuration, System Restore, Recovery Console, ASR

e. System Restore, Last Known Good Configuration, ASR, Recovery Console

5. How can you stop a program that is running in a command prompt window? Choose *two* answers.

   a. Type Exit and press Enter.

   b. Press Ctrl+C.

   c. Press Ctrl+End.

   d. Press Ctrl+Break.

6. You need to create a text file that others cannot see in a public folder. What command do you use to hide the file?

   a. HIDE

   b. COPY

   c. EDIT

   d. ATTRIB

7. A Windows 2000 computer cannot connect to the network. Which command can be used to display the IP configuration of the computer?

   a. Repair

   b. Ipconfig/Display

   c. Ipconfig/All

   d. Winipcfg

8. You need to enable folder encryption on a Windows XP file server. When you open the Properties window for drive C, you discover the drive is using the FAT32 file system. What command can you use before you can enable folder encryption?

   a. CONVERT

   b. ENCRYPT/ON

   c. ATTRIB

   d. FORMAT

9. Lucy is a backup operator responsible for backing up the file server each night. When she arrives at work each morning, the first thing she does is check for any file system errors that occurred the previous night during the backup operation. Which tool does she use to check for these errors?

   a. NTBackup

   b. System Restore

   c. Device Manager

   d. Event Viewer

10. Nathan wants to make his job as a system administrator easier by creating a convenient window where he can quickly access these tools: Device Manager, Event Viewer, Group Policy, and Services. Which tool does he use to create this administrative window?

    a. MMC.exe

    b. Windows.exe

c. Administrative Tools

d. Msconfig.exe

11. You need to set up three folders for user data. The users in the Accounting Department need access to Folder 1. The users in the Payroll Department need access to Folder 2. Users from both departments need access to Folder 3. Which applet in Control Panel allows you to qualify access to a folder by user group?

    a. User Accounts

    b. Administrative Tools

    c. Folder Options

    d. Group Policy

12. You need to set up some folders for user data and control which user group has access to each folder. You decide to create three new user groups. What tool do you use to create these groups?

    a. Group Policy

    b. User Accounts

    c. Event Viewer

    d. Computer Management

13. Jackie complains that his new game is not running fast enough. Which action is *least* likely to improve performance?

    a. Upgrading memory

    b. Converting the file system from NTFS to FAT32

    c. Updating video drivers

    d. Defragging the hard drive

14. A Windows XP installation is corrupted. You are able to boot the system into the Recovery Console. Which command will take you to the folder where Windows is installed?

    a. CD C:/Windows

    b. Systemroot

    c. Logon

    d. Bootcfg/list

15. Matt tells you that his video display is very plain and he cannot change the screen resolution or color quality. Which action allows Matt to update the video drivers?

    a. In Device Manager, right-click the display adapter and select the Driver tab.

    b. In the Display Properties window, select the Advanced button on the Settings tab.

    c. Either answer a or b will work.

    d. You cannot update the video driver. The best thing to do is uninstall the display adapter and reinstall it.

CHAPTER 4

Printers and Scanners

Troubleshooting scenarios in this chapter:

SUMMARY OF DOMAIN CONTENT

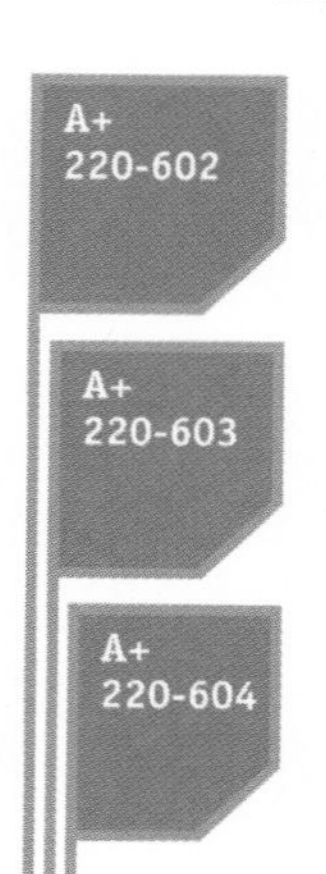

This section of the chapter contains a summary overview of the content in the CompTIA A+ 220-602 Domain 4, *Printers and Scanners*, 220-603 Domain 3, *Printers and Scanners*, and 220-604 Domain 3, *Printers and Scanners*. The high-level objectives for this domain are:

- Identify the fundamental principles of using printers and scanners
- Install, configure, optimize, and upgrade printers and scanners
- Identify tools and diagnostic procedures to troubleshoot printers and scanners
- Perform preventative maintenance of printers and scanners (220-602 and 220-604 only)

IDENTIFY THE FUNDAMENTAL PRINCIPLES OF USING PRINTERS AND SCANNERS

Describe processes used by printers and scanners including laser, ink dispersion, thermal, solid ink, and impact printers and scanners

The laser printer six-step process is (1) cleaning, (2) conditioning, (3) writing, (4) developing, (5) transferring, and (6) fusing. Ink dispersion (inkjet) printers eject ink onto the paper using a matrix of small dots. Thermal printers heat the ink, which then melts onto the paper. One type of thermal printer is a solid ink printer, which stores ink in solid blocks. Dot matrix printers are impact printers, which are the oldest type of printer still used because they can produce multicopy printouts, but are only used for plain text printing. A dot matrix printer uses print wires that strike a ribbon against the paper as tractors pull fan-fold paper through the printer. A flat-bed scanner works by moving the scanning head across the paper, using reflected light converted to electrical signals. Some printers and scanners are combo units, meaning they can serve multiple functions such as a combination printer, scanner, copier, and fax machine.

INSTALL, CONFIGURE, OPTIMIZE, AND UPGRADE PRINTERS AND SCANNERS

Install and configure printers and scanners

- ***Power and connect the device using local or network port***
  Older local printers used parallel ports. Today's local printers use USB, wireless (Bluetooth, infrared, or WiFi), FireWire (IEEE 1394), SCSI, PC Card, or ExpressCard ports or connections. A network printer has a NIC with a network port, and the printer is assigned an IP address on the network. A scanner might use a FireWire (the fastest type of connection), USB, serial, parallel, or SCSI connection. FireWire is managed by the IEEE 1394 standards, and parallel ports are managed by the IEEE 1284 standards.
- ***Install and update the device driver and calibrate the device***
  Install printers and update device drivers using the Windows XP Printers and Faxes window or the Windows 2000 Printers window. You can also install a printer using installation software provided by the printer manufacturer. Follow manufacturer directions for the installation; some require you to install the software first and others tell you to install the device first. Printers can be calibrated using software bundled with the printer.

- *Configure options and default settings*
  All options, add-on hardware components, and settings must be installed or configured for the printer using the Printers and Faxes window or Printers window. Administrative privileges are required. The LPR/LPD protocol is used to receive print jobs from various operating systems (for example, UNIX, Windows, and Mac) using a remote printer over a TCP/IP network.

Install and configure print drivers (e.g., PCL™, Postscript™, GDI)

Installed printer drivers determine how the OS and printer communicate. The OS and printer communicate a page to print using one of these four methods:

  - The OS tells the printer how to build the page using the PostScript language first developed by Adobe Systems.
  - The OS tells the printer how to build the page using the PCL (Printer Control Language) first developed by Hewlett-Packard. High-end printers can sometimes use both PostScript and PCL languages.
  - Windows builds the page using its internal GDI (Graphics Device Interface) component and then sends the completed page to the printer. This is the most common method for low-end inkjet printers.
  - Raw data is sent to the printer. Dotmatrix printers that can only print plain text use this method.

- *Print test page (220-604 only)*
  Print a test page from the printer Properties window, which you access from the Windows XP Printers and Faxes window or the Windows 2000 Printers window to verify the OS and the printer are communicating correctly. Print a test page using controls at the printer to verify the printer itself is working.
- *Validate compatibility with operating system and applications*
  After printing a test page, print from an application to verify the application can print.
- *Educate user about basic functionality*
  The user has access to printer features, options, and hardware add-ons such as bins, stackers, sorters, and staplers by using the tabs on the printer's Properties window when the user prints from within an application. Administrative privileges are required to install and configure a printer, including configuring add-ons, using the Windows 2000 Printers window or the Windows XP Printers and Faxes window.

Install and configure printer upgrades including memory and firmware (220-602 only)

Printer add-on devices include sorters, bins, trays, staplers, mailboxes, hard drives, and memory. Devices are physically installed and then the Printers and Faxes or Printers window is used to configure the printer to use the device. To upgrade printer firmware, download the upgrade from the printer manufacturer Web site and use firmware on the printer to install the update. Some printers require you to install a replacement DIMM that contains a ROM chip to upgrade the firmware.

Optimize scanner performance including resolution, file format, and default settings (220-602 and 220-603 only)

Resolution, file formats, and other settings are all configured using the scanner software installed on the PC. The higher the resolution (in dpi or dots per inch), the better image quality and larger file size. Possible file formats for pictures are JPEG, PNG, BMP, CVR, DCX, FPX, GIF, PCX, PDF, and TIFF. JPEG files generally offer the most compression (lossy compression) and smaller file size. PNG files use lossless compression, retaining full image quality. Text files can be saved in the TXT, RTF, and PDF formats. The G3 format is used by fax machines for transmitting data. TWAIN is a protocol used between the scanner and PC.

IDENTIFY TOOLS AND DIAGNOSTIC PROCEDURES TO TROUBLESHOOT PRINTERS AND SCANNERS

Gather information about printer/scanner problems

Open the printer window to see the queue of print jobs. LCD panels on the front of printers show error messages.

Review and analyze collected data

Use collected data about the problem to make your best guess if the problem is software or hardware related.

Isolate and resolve identified printer/scanner problems including defining the cause, applying the fix, and verifying functionality

A printer software problem can be caused by the file being printed, the application, the operating system, or installed device drivers. A printer hardware problem can be caused by the printer cable and its connections, the power source, or the printer including the printer memory.

Troubleshoot a print failure (e.g., lack of paper, clear queue, restart print spooler, recycle power on printer, inspect for jams, check for visual indicators) (220-603 only)

Clear the printer queue. Try printing a test page from the Printers and Faxes window. If that fails, try printing a test page using buttons on the printer. Reboot the PC and turn the printer off and back on. Verify the printer is online.

Identify appropriate tools used for troubleshooting and repairing printer/scanner problems (220-602 and 220-604 only)

- *Multimeter*
  Used to test a fuse or verify that a cable is good.
- *Screwdrivers*
  Used to install memory, a hard drive, or other add-on printer component.
- *Cleaning solutions*
  - Generally, don't use cleaning solutions to clean a printer unless specifically told to do so in printer documentation. Use a soft dry cloth to clean the inside of a printer.
  - Some inkjet printers have an overflow tank for ink, which can be emptied by soaking up the ink with a paper towel. Clean spilled ink with a paper towel dampened with water.
- *Extension magnet*
  This is a soft brush that attracts toner to clean the inside of a printer or clean up a toner spill.
- *Test patterns*
  Print a diagnostic test page that can be used to calibrate printer output.

PERFORM PREVENTATIVE MAINTENANCE OF PRINTERS AND SCANNERS (220-602 AND 220-604 ONLY)

Perform scheduled maintenance according to vendor guidelines (e.g., install maintenance kits, reset page counts)

Maintenance kits for laser printers can include rollers, the transfer roller assembly, and the fuser assembly. Install all parts following manufacturer instructions. The instructions also include how to reset the page counter that indicates when the next maintenance is required.

Ensure a suitable environment

Printers and scanners work better in a dust-free environment away from direct sunlight.

Use recommended supplies

Use paper, toner, ink, and maintenance kits supplied or recommended by the printer manufacturer. Recycled supplies such as a recycled toner cartridge can degrade print quality.

SCENARIO 4.1: TROUBLESHOOT PRINTER PROBLEMS

OBJECTIVES

The goal of this lab is to help you learn how to troubleshoot printers. After completing this lab, you will be able to:

- Investigate and solve printer problems.

MATERIALS REQUIRED

This lab requires the following:

- Laser printer
- A Windows XP computer designated for this lab
- Internet access

LAB PREPARATION

Before the lab begins, the instructor or lab assistant needs to do the following:

- Verify that the printer, printer drivers on CD or other media, and Windows XP computer are available.
- Verify that Internet access is available.

SCENARIO BACKGROUND

Every office needs at least one printer, probably more than one, and PC support technicians are expected to know how to install, maintain, and troubleshoot printers. Most local printers today use a USB or FireWire port to connect to a PC or they use a wireless connection. Network printers that connect directly to the network using a network cable are excellent solutions for businesses. In this lab, you learn about all kinds of printers and what you can do to maintain them and solve problems when they don't work.

ESTIMATED COMPLETION TIME: 45 minutes

SCENARIO AND TROUBLESHOOTING

Caution

When servicing printers, know that the laser beam inside a laser printer and the bright light inside a scanner can harm your eyes. Unplug a printer or scanner before opening it for service. Also, the fuser assembly of laser printers and the print head of dot matrix printers get very hot, so you should always allow a printer to cool down before opening it. Because of the danger of charged capacitors, don't work inside a laser printer wearing an antistatic bracelet. Toner in a laser printer can stain clothes; the toner sets with heat so be sure to clean clothes with cool water. You can pick up stray toner off the floor or inside a printer with a magnetic brush, dry cloth, or vacuum. Don't use water or compressed air to clean up toner because water can smear the toner and damage the printer, and compressed air can spread the toner. Dry paper particles and dust can be removed from inside a printer using a soft dry cloth, compressed air, or a vacuum. Also, many printer manufacturers warn to not use ammonia-based cleaners on or around a printer.

Research and answer the following questions about supporting printers:

1. Julie has just purchased a Canon Pixma iP6220D inkjet printer. She connected it to her notebook computer using her USB port, and it works fine. However, she understands the printer can be connected wirelessly. Answer the following questions:
   - What type of wireless technology does the printer use?

     ____

   - What optional part do you need to make the printer wireless?

     ____

   - Julie's notebook does not support Bluetooth. Suggest a device she can purchase that will use a USB port and allow her to connect her printer wirelessly. Print a Web page showing the product. What is the total cost of parts to make the printer-to-notebook wireless connection?

     ____

2. Users are complaining that the office laser printer is showing signs of wear. Printouts are faded and sometimes show specks, lines, and smeared toner. You try replacing the toner cartridge, but the problem still persists. Next you try to clean the printer. Search your printer documentation and/or the printer manufacturer Web site for instructions to clean the printer.
   - From the menu of some printers, you can direct the printer to print a self-cleaning page. If your printer has this option, do so now.
   - If the problem is not resolved, the next step is to clean the inside of the printer. Before you start, turn off the printer, unplug it, and allow it to cool. As you work, be sure not to touch the soft transfer roller. Skin oils on the roller can affect print quality. What other cautions (if any) do the instructions give to keep you from damaging the printer or hurting yourself?

     ____

- Clean the inside of your printer and list the high-level steps below.

3. The printer problem is still not solved, so you decide to check if it is time to install a maintenance kit. Answer the following questions about your laser printer:
   - What is the current page count of your printer?
   - At what page count does the manufacturer suggest you install a maintenance kit?
   - What is the part number of the maintenance kit and how much does it cost?
   - Search the printer documentation and/or the printer manufacturer Web site for the instructions to install the maintenance kit. List the parts in the kit.
4. Printers sometimes get paper jams. Following instructions for your laser printer, open and inspect all the compartments, input trays, output areas, and feeders as specified in your printer instructions. List below all areas you inspected:

REVIEW QUESTIONS

1. Why is it important to reset the page counter after you install a printer maintenance kit?
2. Name three types of wireless technologies used by printers.
3. What device is especially designed to pick up loose toner?
4. Which protocol is likely to be used when a Windows XP PC sends a print job over the Internet?

SCENARIO 4.2: INSTALL AND USE A SCANNER

OBJECTIVES

The goal of this lab is to help you learn how to support scanners. After completing this lab, you will be able to:

- Install and use a scanner.
- Configure scanner settings for optimum file size and format.

MATERIALS REQUIRED

This lab requires the following:

- Scanner and scanner drivers
- A Windows XP computer designated for this lab
- Internet access

LAB PREPARATION

Before the lab begins, the instructor or lab assistant needs to do the following:

- Verify the scanner, scanner drivers on CD or other media, and Windows XP computer are available.
- Verify that Internet access is available.

SCENARIO BACKGROUND

PC support technicians need to be able to install, configure, and troubleshoot scanners. As part of your job of supporting users and the challenges they encounter, you need to be able to help them decide on the optimum file format to use for scanned files. You need to know which formats work best to compress data without losing image quality, especially when files are transmitted over the Internet or used to build Web sites. You learn about all these skills in this lab.

ESTIMATED COMPLETION TIME: 45 minutes

SCENARIO AND TROUBLESHOOTING

As a freelance PC support technician, you enjoy working for a variety of people and companies, but your greatest challenge is to learn about all kinds of software and hardware as you face the next client's problem. Susan, a graphics artist, has asked for your help with installing and using her new scanner. Using your scanner, do the following:

1. What is the name and model number of your scanner?

   ____

2. If your scanner is not already installed, install it now following manufacturer directions.
   - What type of connection does the scanner use? (for example, USB)

     ____

   - Do you first install the software or connect the scanner to the PC?

     ____

- Does the scanner include OCR software?

____

3. Identify all the buttons or controls on your scanner. Figure 4-1 shows the buttons on the front of one scanner, which all use scanner software installed on the PC. List each button on your scanner with a brief description:

____

____

____

____

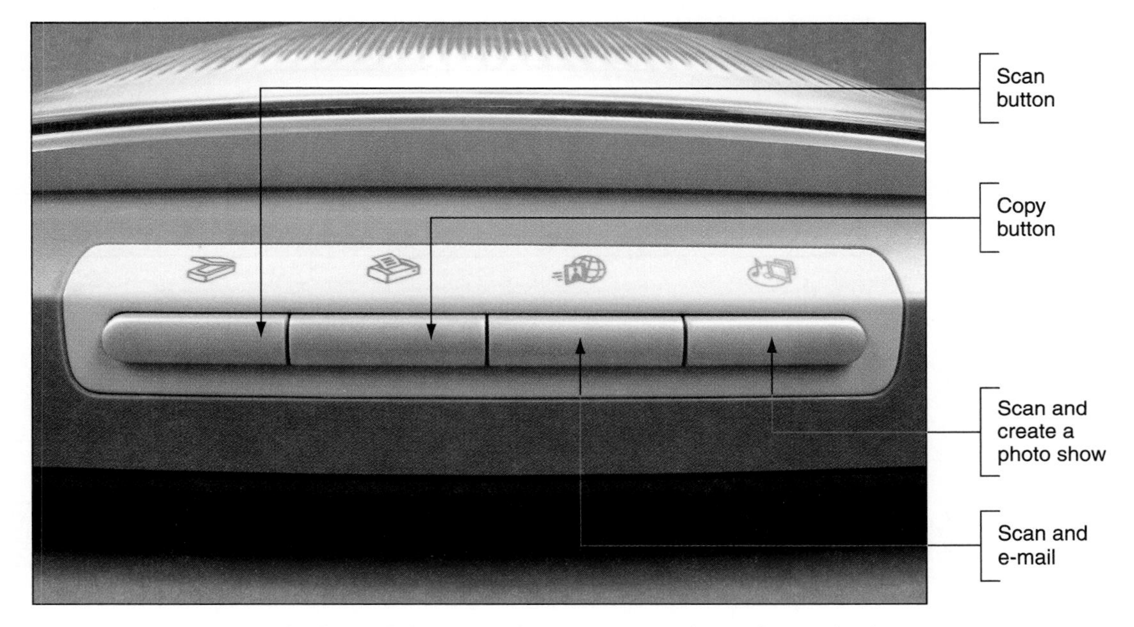

Figure 4-1 Buttons on the front of the HP Scanjet 3970 scanner by Hewlett-Packard

4. Scan a drawing, photo, or document using the scan button on the scanner.
5. Scan another drawing, photo, or document using the software on the PC.
6. If your scanner has a Copy button, use it to copy a picture or document to your printer.
7. List the file formats that your scanner supports:

____

____

____

____

When scanning an image and saving it to a file, you must select the resolution and file type; the appropriate choices depend on how the image will be used. The highest resolutions are not normally used unless you are scanning a very small picture that you need to enlarge.

High resolutions can make the file size huge, slowing down printing and file transmission. When publishing an image to the Web, small file size is important, but not so small that image quality suffers. When images are printed (especially for published printing), relatively higher resolutions and file types that don't sacrifice image quality are needed.

Now investigate which resolutions and file types produce the smallest size file for the best quality image. Follow these directions:

1. Select a graphic or photo to test that is rather complex with variation of colors.
2. What resolution is your scanner currently using?

   ____

3. Set your scanner resolution to its lowest possible value.
4. Scan the picture, saving the image using three of the file formats your scanner supports. List the filename and size of the three files:

   ____

   ____

   ____

   ____

5. Set your scanner resolution to its highest possible value.
6. Rescan the picture, saving the image using the same three file formats. If you get an error, try reducing the resolution. List the filename and size of the three new files:

   ____

   ____

   ____

   ____

7. Display each of the eight images on screen. Zoom in on each image. Can you detect a difference in image quality? Note any differences.

   ____

   ____

8. Based on what you have learned, which file format would you recommend to a user building a Web site? Why?

   ____

   ____

9. Reset the scanner resolution to the value recorded in Step 2.

REVIEW QUESTIONS

1. Does the JPEG file format use lossy or lossless compression? Does the PNG file format use lossy or lossless compression?

   ____

2. Which file format is used for text: RTF or BMP?

   ____

3. Which protocol is used when the PC and scanner are communicating: TWAIN, TIFF, or LPD/LPR?

   ____

4. Order these three file types from smallest to largest file size: PNG, BMP, JPEG.

   ____

5. Why would you choose to use the PNG file format over JPEG? Over BMP?

   ____

PRACTICE EXAM

The following practice exam covers the domain, *Printers and Scanners*. Answers to the odd-numbered questions are provided in Appendix B.

1. When a printer experiences frequent paper jams, which of the following might be the problem? Select all answers that apply.
   - **a.** The toner cartridge is low on toner
   - **b.** The inside of the printer is dirty
   - **c.** The fuser assembly needs replacing
   - **d.** The guide rollers inside the paper trays are not aligned
   - **e.** The paper is damp or the room is too humid
   - **f.** A paper tray is overloaded with paper
2. Which step in the laser printing process is responsible for putting a uniform electrical charge on the surface of the drum?
   - **a.** Transferring
   - **b.** Cleaning
   - **c.** Developing
   - **d.** Conditioning
   - **e.** Writing
3. A dot matrix printer is printing with fading at the top of each letter it prints. What action is most likely to fix the problem?
   - **a.** Installing a new printer ribbon
   - **b.** Recalibrating the position and angle of the print head
   - **c.** Cleaning the printer
   - **d.** Reinstalling the printer drivers

4. Which component on a laser printer is likely to get the hottest?
   a. The print head
   b. The fuser assembly
   c. The paper tray
   d. The paper guide rollers
5. Mary wants to use the office laser printer as a duplexing printer, but she cannot find an option on her Printers window to print on both sides of the paper. She has looked at another user's computer and saw that it does have the duplexing option. How do you fix her problem?
   a. Reinstall the printer drivers with the duplexing option enabled.
   b. Using the control panel on the front of the printer, configure the printer to enable duplexing.
   c. On the Configure tab of the printer Properties window, check Duplexing Unit.
   d. Instruct Mary that duplexing is only allowed for users that have administrative privileges and she does not have those privileges.
6. Jack wants to configure the office printer to install a new envelope feeder, but when he opens the printer Properties window, he discovers that the option to install the feeder is grayed out so he cannot make a change. What is Jack's problem?
   a. The printer Properties window is not needed to install a new envelope feeder. Jack only needs to enable the feeder using the printer's control panel menus.
   b. Jack's user account does not have administrative privileges. Someone needs to log on as an administrator to perform the operation.
   c. If the option to install the feeder is grayed out, this laser printer cannot use an envelope feeder.
   d. The printer drivers are not installed correctly. Jack needs to reinstall the drivers.
7. An inkjet printer prints with faded and strange colors. Which of the following is likely the problem? Choose *two* answers.
   a. The printer drivers need updating
   b. The printer is short on memory
   c. The printer needs calibrating using software from the printer manufacturer
   d. The ink cartridges need replacing
   e. The color quality in the Display Properties window needs adjusting
8. Using a scanner, you can scan a page using which method or methods? (Choose all that apply.)
   a. Press a button on the scanner or use an application installed on the computer
   b. Press a button on the scanner or use Control Panel under Windows
   c. Press a button on the scanner or use scanner software installed on the PC
   d. Use the Scanner icon in Control Panel or use the Printers and Faxes window

9. Which protocol is used when a scanner sends a scanned image to a computer?
   a. TCP/IP
   b. TWAIN
   c. LPR/LPD
   d. Postscript
10. A computer is most likely to use which protocol when communicating a print job to a network laser printer?
    a. Postscript or PCL
    b. GDI or G3
    c. TWAIN
    d. PDF
11. Which file format is best used to retain the best possible image quality while keeping the file size as small as possible?
    a. BMP
    b. JPEG
    c. PNG
    d. GIF
12. Jill is unable to print to the network printer. When you print a test page using controls at the printer, you discover the IP address of the printer is the same as the IP address of Jill's computer. You try restarting both Jill's computer and the printer, but the problem does not change. How do you best fix the problem?
    a. On Jill's computer, reinstall the printer so that it uses static IP addressing. Assign an IP address to the printer that is different from the computer's IP address.
    b. Using the Printers and Faxes window of Jill's computer, reconfigure the printer so that it uses MAC addressing to communicate on the network rather than IP addressing.
    c. Exchange the NIC in the printer.
    d. Change the IP address of Jill's computer so that you can access the network printer. Then set the printer to use a static IP address that is different from other devices on the network.
13. A USB printer is connected directly to John's computer. Others on the network want to use this printer. What is the best solution to make the printer accessible to all users?
    a. Install a wireless adapter in the printer's USB port so that others can use the printer wirelessly.
    b. On John's computer, share the printer so that others on the network can access it as a network printer.
    c. Move the printer to a central location in the building. Install a network adapter in the USB port and connect the printer directly to the network.
    d. Buy a new network printer that works just like John's printer.

14. Ann's old dot matrix printer uses a parallel port. She wants to make sure the printer's performance is as good as it can be. Which action is likely to help?
    a. In CMOS setup, change the configuration of the parallel port to use a DMA channel
    b. Exchange the printer's print head
    c. In Windows, use the Chkdsk command on drive C
    d. Clean the printer and replace the printer ribbon
15. Jane cannot print to her local printer. When you try to print a test page using controls at the printer, the page prints with no problem. What have you proven?
    a. The problem is with the printer drivers
    b. The problem is with the application from which Jane is printing
    c. The problem is not the printer itself
    d. The problem is not with the printer cable or its connections

CHAPTER 5

Networks

Troubleshooting scenarios in this chapter:

- **Scenario 5.1:** Troubleshoot Network Problems
- **Scenario 5.2:** Secure a Wireless Network
- **Scenario 5.3:** Understand the OSI Model

SUMMARY OF DOMAIN CONTENT

A+
220-603

This section of the chapter contains a summary overview of the content in the CompTIA A+ 220-602 Domain 5, *Networks* and 220-603 Domain 4, *Networks*. Please note that the CompTIA A+ 220-604 exam does not include the *Networks* domain. The high-level objectives for this domain are:

- Identify the fundamental principles of networks
- Install, configure, optimize, and upgrade networks
- Use tools and diagnostic procedures to troubleshoot network problems
- Perform preventive maintenance on networks, including securing and protecting network cabling (220-602 only)

IDENTIFY THE FUNDAMENTAL PRINCIPLES OF NETWORKS

***Identify names, purposes, and characteristics of basic network protocols and terminologies. For example*:**

- *ISP*
  An ISP (Internet service provider) is a commercial group such as AOL and Earthlink that provides Internet access for a monthly fee.
- *TCP/IP (e.g., gateway, subnet mask, DNS, WINS, static and automatic address assignment)*
  TCP/IP is a suite of networking protocols (or languages) used for communication over the Internet and most private networks. TCP is responsible for guaranteed data delivery, and IP is responsible for routing.

  The gateway is the IP address of the computer or device that stands between two networks. The subnet mask is a group of 32 bits that defines whether another computer is on the local or remote network. DNS and WINS servers are used to track domain names to IP addresses. A static IP address is manually assigned to a computer or other device on the network. An automatic IP address is assigned when the computer cannot acquire a dynamic IP address from the DHCP server.

Note

Networking technologies use a lot of acronyms. For a complete listing of CompTIA A+ Acronyms, including those used in this book, see Appendix A.

- *IPX/SPX (NWLink)*
  A suite of networking protocols first used by Novell NetWare, similar to TCP/IP. NWLink is Microsoft's version of IPX/SPX; it is used by a Windows PC on an IPX/SPX private network.
- *NETBEUI/NETBIOS*
  NetBEUI is an outdated networking protocol by Microsoft that does not support routing. NetBIOS is an API protocol used by applications on a NetBEUI network. It is similar to Windows Sockets on a TCP/IP network.
- *SMTP*
  The protocol used to send e-mail over the Internet. SMTP AUTH is a variation of SMTP and authenticates that a client has the right to use the e-mail server.
- *IMAP*
  An e-mail protocol that controls downloading e-mail to the client. IMAP replaces the earlier POP protocol; the current IMAP version is IMAP4.

- *HTML*
  A markup language used to create Web pages and other hypertext documents.
- *HTTP*
  A communications protocol used by the World Wide Web.
- *HTTPS*
  "HTTPS" appears in the browser address box when data is being transmitted using an encryption method. The "S" in HTTPS indicates a secure site and implies a digital certificate has authenticated the site.
- *SSL*
  SSL (Secure Sockets Layer) is an encryption method that uses a digital certificate; it is the most popular encryption method used on the Web. TLS (Transport Layer Security) and PCT (Private Communication Technology) are two other encryption methods, both stronger than SSL. Internet Explorer supports all three methods.
- *Telnet*
  Telnet is an outdated command-line interface between two computers on a network. Telnet was first used on UNIX computers. Telnet uses port number 23, which can be written as TCP:23.
- *FTP*
  A protocol and service used to transfer files over the Internet or other IP network. FTP uses port numbers 20 and 21, which can be written as TCP:20 and TCP:21.
- *DNS*
  The DNS (Domain Name System) tracks domain names and their corresponding IP addresses.

Identify names, purposes, and characteristics of technologies for establishing connectivity. For example:

- *Dial-up networking*
  A method for connecting to a network or to another computer that uses two modems and regular phone lines for communication. It is the slowest and least expensive way to connect to the Internet.
- *Broadband (e.g., DSL, cable, satellite)*
  Broadband is a transmission method that carries more than one type of data on the same medium. DSL is a high-speed data transmission method used to access the Internet that shares regular phone lines with telephones. A cable modem shares a cable with cable TV. Satellite broadband uses two-way communication between a dish on your roof and the satellite.
- *ISDN Networking*
  ISDN is an older broadband technology that uses regular phone lines. It has mostly been replaced by DSL.
- *Wireless (all 802.11)*
  IEEE 802.11, also known as Wi-Fi, is a group of protocols (802.11a/b/g/n) used for wireless transmissions. Wi-Fi is the most popular wireless technology for local networks. 802.11g and 802.11b use a frequency range of 2.4 GHz. 802.11g runs at 54 Mbps, and 802.11b runs at 11 Mbps. 802.11a runs at 54 Mbps and is not compatible with 802.11b/g because it runs in the 5.0 GHz range. 802.11n is the latest Wi-Fi technology; it improves the speed of 802.11g by using multiple antennas for multiple simultaneous transmissions (called multiple-input multiple-out or MIMO).
- *LAN/WAN*
  A PAN (personal area network) is used for personal devices at close range. One technology used for a PAN is Bluetooth. A LAN (local area network) covers a small local area

and most likely uses Ethernet and Wi-Fi technology. A MAN (metropolitan area network) covers a large campus or city, and can use Ethernet with fiber-optic cable. A WAN (wide area network) covers a wide geographical network and can use a variety of technologies, such as Ethernet, 802.11g/n, Gigabit Ethernet, ATM, T-Carrier (T1 through T5), and SONET. SONET backbones make use of different OC levels (OC-1 through OC-768).

- *Infrared*
  An older wireless technology that uses infrared light over a PAN. For infrared communication, there must be an unobstructed view between infrared devices.
- *Bluetooth*
  A popular PAN technology that uses encryption and is slower than Wi-Fi. Bluetooth is replacing infrared as the technology for wireless short-range PANs.
- *Cellular*
  A network, such as that used by cell phones, which covers a large geographical area by using one base station in each cell of the network.
- *VoIP*
  VoIP (Voice over IP) uses the Internet for voice transmission and can connect to regular phone lines to provide seamless phone service.

INSTALL, CONFIGURE, OPTIMIZE, AND UPGRADE NETWORKS

Install and configure browsers (220-602 only)

- *Enable/disable script support*
  For best browser security, disable all script support or configure the browser to prompt the user before a script is executed. Changes in Internet Explorer are made in the Internet Options window.
- *Configure proxy and security settings*
  Internet Explorer security settings are made in the Internet Options window. If your network has only one proxy server, IE will find it without requiring you to specify it.

Establish network connectivity

- *Install and configure network cards*
  - After the NIC and drivers are installed, the lights on the back of the NIC indicate activity.
  - Configure TCP/IP to use static or dynamic IP addressing. For static IP addressing, you need to specify an IP address, a subnet mask, a default gateway address, and at least one DNS server address.
  - Use the Ping command to confirm connectivity.
- *Obtain a connection*
  Using the Windows XP Network Connections window, display the properties of the local area connection, which should verify that the NIC is bound to the Internet Protocol (TCP/IP) and other protocols used by the network. For wireless networks, consider that the wireless LAN might be secured and require a passphrase, or that the wireless NIC's MAC address should be given to the network administrator.
- *Configure client options (e.g., Microsoft and Novell) and network options (e.g., domain, workgroup, and tree)*
  For a TCP/IP network, the NIC must be bound to the Internet Protocol. For a Novell IPX/SPX network, the NIC must be bound to the NWLink protocol. In Windows XP,

enter the domain or workgroup name in the Computer Name tab of the System Properties window.

- *Configure network options*
  You can create a network drive map using Windows Explorer. Share files and folders using their properties windows.

Demonstrate the ability to share network resources

- *Models*
  Using a peer-to-peer model (called a workgroup in Windows), a group of computers share the responsibilities of managing resources on a network. Using the client-server model (called a domain in Windows), one computer on the network manages the sharing of resources for all computers on the network. Examples of server operating systems are Windows Server 2003, UNIX, Linux, and Novell NetWare.
- *Configure permissions*
  An administrator can control user account rights or permissions using the User Accounts applet or the Administrative Tools applet in Control Panel. Permissions can also be configured using Group Policy. If simple file sharing is disabled, an administrator can control which group or user account has access to a file, folder, or printer. Use the Computer Management window in the Administrative Tools console to create and manage user groups.
- *Capacities/limitations for sharing for each operating system*
  - Using an NTFS volume, you can compress files, folders, and the entire volume; apply disk quotas; encrypt files and folders, and make your user folders private. Two Windows components are needed to share resources: Client for Microsoft Networks and File and Printer Sharing.
  - For Windows XP Professional, to gain better control over configuring permissions for files and folders, disable simple file sharing in the Folder Options window. (This option is not available in Windows XP Home Edition.) Share files, folders, and printers using their properties windows to assign permissions to individual users and user groups.

USE TOOLS AND DIAGNOSTIC PROCEDURES TO TROUBLESHOOT NETWORK PROBLEMS

Identify names, purposes, and characteristics of tools. For example:

- *Command-line tools (e.g., IPCONFIG.EXE, PING.EXE, TRACERT.EXE, and NSLOOKUP.EXE)*
  IPConfig is used to view connection data and to release and renew an IP address. Ping is used to test for connectivity. Tracert is used to trace the path of data packets. Nslookup displays information about the DNS service.
- *Cable testing device (220-602 only)*
  Use a two-piece cable tester to verify that a cable is good. You can also use it to trace network cables through a building.

Diagnose and troubleshoot basic network issues. For example:

- *Driver/network interface*
  Use Device Manager to look for problems with the NIC's drivers and test the NIC. Use lights on the NIC and the Ping command to verify connectivity. Use the Windows

XP Network Connections window or the Windows 2000/XP IPConfig command to repair the connection.

- *Protocol configuration*
  - ***TCP/IP (e.g., gateway, subnet mask, DNS, WINS, static and automatic address assignment)***
    When using static IP addressing, assign values to the IP address, default gateway, subnet mask, and DNS servers. When using dynamic IP addressing, if the computer is not able to lease an IP address from a DHCP server, it will revert to alternate IP configuration settings that you have specified on the Alternate Configuration tab of the Internet Protocol (TCP/IP) Properties window. The default setting on this window is to use an automatic private IP address. However, you can specific static IP address values.
  - *IPX/SPX (NWLink)*
    Bind a NIC to the NWLink protocol using the Local Area Connection Properties window.
- *Permissions*
  Use previously mentioned tools to prevent or allow certain user accounts to read, write, or change files in certain folders shared on the network.
- *Firewall configuration*
  A hardware firewall is stronger than a software firewall. Always have a firewall turned on to protect a computer or network. Note that the firewall might need to be configured to allow certain incoming, unsolicited traffic to the computer or network.
- *Electrical interference*
  Electromagnetic interference (EMI) can undermine network performance. A ferrite clamp is a clamp placed near the connector on a network cable and is used to eliminate EMI. Fluorescent lighting, heavy equipment, and snarled cabling can cause EMI. 802.11 wireless networks can be affected by EMI. Shielded twisted pair cabling offers better protection against EMI but is more expensive than unshielded twisted pair. Fiber-optic cabling is not affected by EMI.

PERFORM PREVENTIVE MAINTENANCE ON NETWORKS, INCLUDING SECURING AND PROTECTING NETWORK CABLING (220-602 ONLY)

Install a ferrite clamp as needed to eliminate interference on a network cable. Make sure that cabling is out of harm's way so that it will not be stepped on or tripped over. Frayed or damaged cabling should be replaced. For the best protection against EMI and cable damage, install cabling in a dedicated conduit, and don't put phone lines in the same conduit. Use plenum-grade cabling between floors of buildings.

SCENARIO 5.1: TROUBLESHOOT NETWORK PROBLEMS

OBJECTIVES

The goal of this lab is to help you learn how to troubleshoot problems with networks using a variety of tools and methods. After completing this lab, you will be able to:

- Use troubleshooting utilities and tools to solve a variety of network problems.

MATERIALS REQUIRED

This lab requires the following:

- A Windows XP computer designated for this lab
- A small network using a router that connects to the Internet using DSL or cable modem

LAB PREPARATION

Before the lab begins, the instructor or lab assistant needs to do the following:

- Make a Windows XP computer available.
- Verify that Internet access is available by way of a small router.
- Verify that documentation for the router is available or can be downloaded from the Internet.

SCENARIO BACKGROUND

Almost every modern office or home computer has Internet access, and most of these computers are also connected to a small or large network. A PC support technician must know how to set up a small network, connect a computer or network to the Internet, and maintain the network and Internet connection. This lab assumes that you have already practiced these skills and takes you forward toward learning how to solve network problems. Most often, network problems are easy to solve, and only require checking simple things like cable connections or expired IP addresses. In this lab, you learn how to troubleshoot network and Internet problems using a variety of tools and methods.

ESTIMATED COMPLETION TIME: 1 hour

SCENARIO

Tracy works for a large corporation that has several branch offices in his city. His job as a PC support technician is to roam among the branch offices, solving any computer or network problems as they arise. The company uses a large centralized database that employees can access over the Internet using their Web browsers. The interface and security of the database is managed by Citrix Web Client, which is third-party application delivery software. In addition, some branch offices have a local file server. Each branch office has its own access to the Internet by way of cable modem or DSL.

In the following troubleshooting section, you learn about some of the problems that Tracy faces on a typical day at a small branch office.

TROUBLESHOOTING

When Tracy arrives at work, users tell him the network is down. The network has six computers connected to a router that also connects to a cable modem. When troubleshooting any network problem, as with most computer problems, it helps to find out what works and what does not. List the first three things Tracy should check.

____

____

____

Tracy has discovered that three computers don't have network access. Therefore, he decides to check the router that also serves as a switch for the network. Using your computer, router, network, and DSL box or cable modem, answer the following questions and follow these directions:

1. What is the IP address of your router on the local network?

 ____

2. Enter the router's IP address in your browser address box to access the router firmware. Firmware utilities differ from one manufacturer to another; Figure 5-1 shows the main Setup window for one Linksys router.

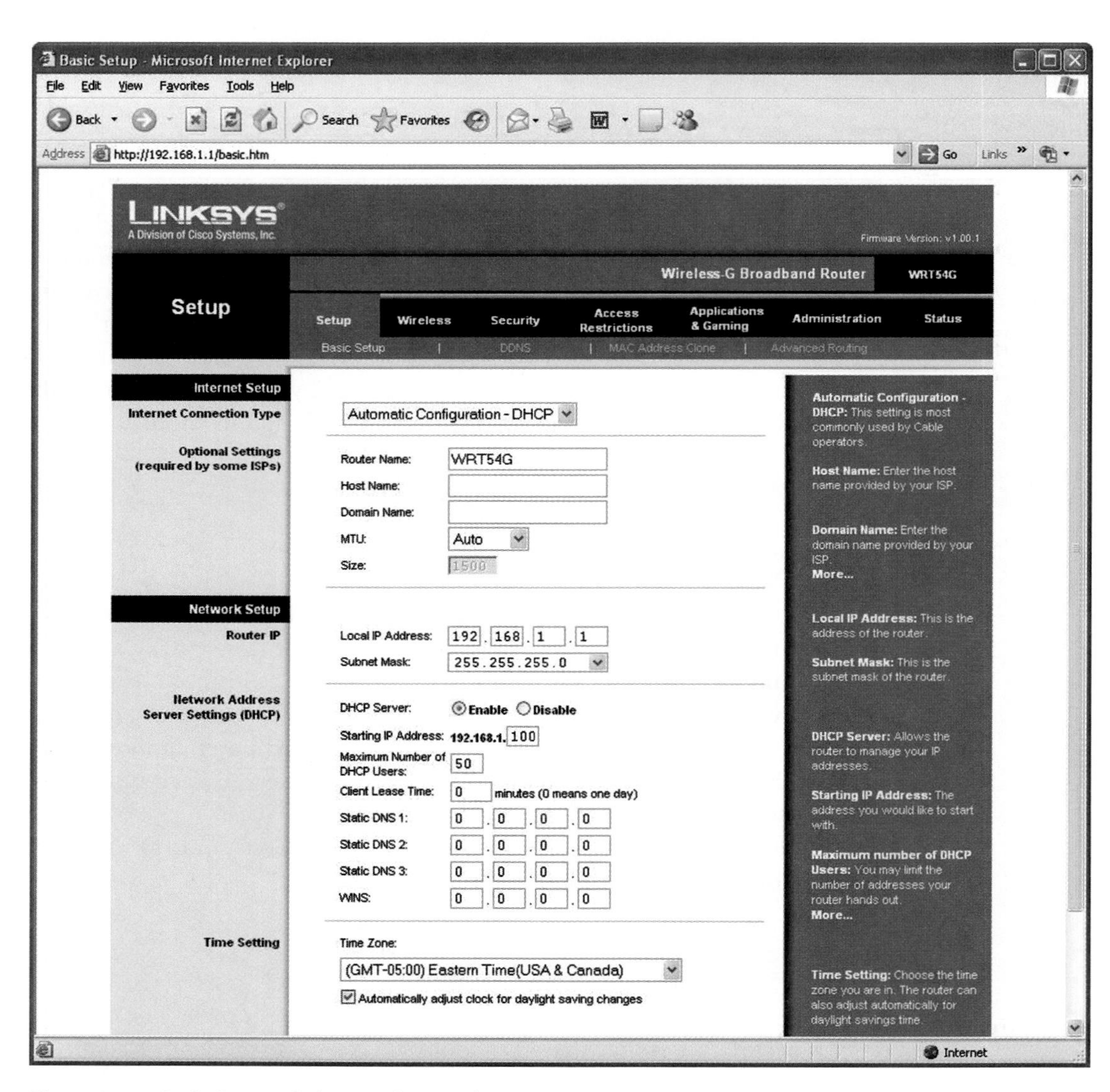

Figure 5-1 Basic Setup window used to configure a Linksys router

Answer these questions:

- Is the router using static or dynamic IP addressing to your ISP? What is the IP address of the router on the ISP network?

  ____

- Why is it necessary for the router to have two IP addresses?

  ____

- Does your router have firewall abilities? If so, which router setting enables the firewall to block anonymous Internet requests to the local network?

  ____

- Does your router have the ability to be a DHCP server for your local network? If so, what is the maximum number of DHCP users the network can have?

  ____

3. Reset your router by turning it off and then turning it back on.
4. Using a computer on your network, release and renew the IP address of this computer. What is the new IP address?

   ____

Tracy verifies that each computer on the network has access to network resources, that each computer can access the Internet, and that all appears to work well. Later that day, a user named Sandra tells Tracy that she cannot access the Internet. Do the following:

1. Reorder the following actions in the sequence you should perform them to fix the problem:

   ____

   a. Reboot the user's PC.
   b. Power down the DSL or cable modem box.
   c. Check whether other computers on the network have a similar problem.
   d. Release and renew the PC's IP address.
   e. Power down the router.
   f. Power up the router.
   g. Power up the DSL or cable modem box.
2. After following the preceding steps, other users on the network have Internet access, but Sandra still does not. Reorder the following actions in the sequence you should perform them to fix the problem:

   ____

   a. Check the lights on the back of the NIC.
   b. Uninstall and reinstall the NIC drivers.

c. Verify that Sandra can access resources on the network, such as shared folders and printers.

d. Check Device Manager for errors.

e. Replace the NIC.

Gary is using his new laptop computer for the first time, and asks you for help. He cannot connect to the local file server. He is also accustomed to seeing the file server as drive K in Windows Explorer. The Map Network Drive window appears in Figure 5-2. The file server is named File_Server and the shared folder is named Shared_Files.

Figure 5-2 Map Network Drive window

- What menu in Windows Explorer do you use to access the Map Network Drive window?

  ____

- What entry should appear in the Folder drop-down list in this window? Test your answer by mapping a network drive to a shared folder on your network.

  ____

- Without using a mapped network drive, what can Gary enter into the Run dialog box to access this folder? Test your answer by accessing a shared folder on your network using the Run dialog box.

  ____

The same afternoon, Tracy returns from lunch to find out that no one in the office has Internet access. He resets the router but the problem persists. Reorder the following steps to reset the cable modem and the router:

____

1. Turn on the cable modem.
2. Turn off the cable modem.
3. Turn off the router.
4. Turn on the router.
5. Wait for the cable modem lights to settle down.

Leslie tells you she needs to participate in a demonstration of third-party video conferencing software the company is considering for purchase. The vendor's technical support staff, which is responsible for setting up the demonstration, needs you to open port 3090 on her computer so they can access her computer from the Internet for the demonstration. Even though opening a port is a security risk, it only needs to be open for one day. Using your router and a computer on your network, list the steps to open the port to this Windows XP computer:

____

____

____

____

____

REVIEW QUESTIONS

1. When mapping a network drive to a folder named Jason on a computer named Mary, what is the full path to the network drive?

   ____

2. How many backslashes should you have used in the answer to Question 1?

   ____

3. Which is faster: Bluetooth or Wi-Fi?

   ____

4. How many times faster is USB 2.0 than USB 1.1?

   ____

5. How must a folder on a file server be configured before you can access it with a network drive map?

   ____

SCENARIO 5.2: SECURE A WIRELESS NETWORK

OBJECTIVES

The goal of this lab is to help you learn how to secure a wireless network. After completing this lab, you will be able to:

- Set up a wireless network.
- Secure a wireless network.

MATERIALS REQUIRED

This lab requires the following:

- A Windows XP computer with wireless capability designated for this lab
- A wireless access point, such as a multipurpose router

LAB PREPARATION

Before the lab begins, the instructor or lab assistant needs to do the following:

- Make sure that each student or workgroup has access to a Windows XP computer with wireless capability.
- Make a wireless access point available for each student or workgroup.

SCENARIO BACKGROUND

Wireless networks must be secured to prevent unauthorized network use and to prevent hackers from stealing data from the network for illegal or malicious activity. In this lab, you learn several ways you can secure a wireless network.

ESTIMATED COMPLETION TIME: 1 hour

SCENARIO

When you first set up a wireless network, you configure the wireless access point to use the security features. A wireless access point connects to a computer or wired network by way of a USB or network cable. The access point device is configured using this wired connection by entering the IP address of the device in your browser. For example, when you enter the IP address of one Linksys access point in a browser, you can access the Wireless setup utility shown in Figure 5-3.

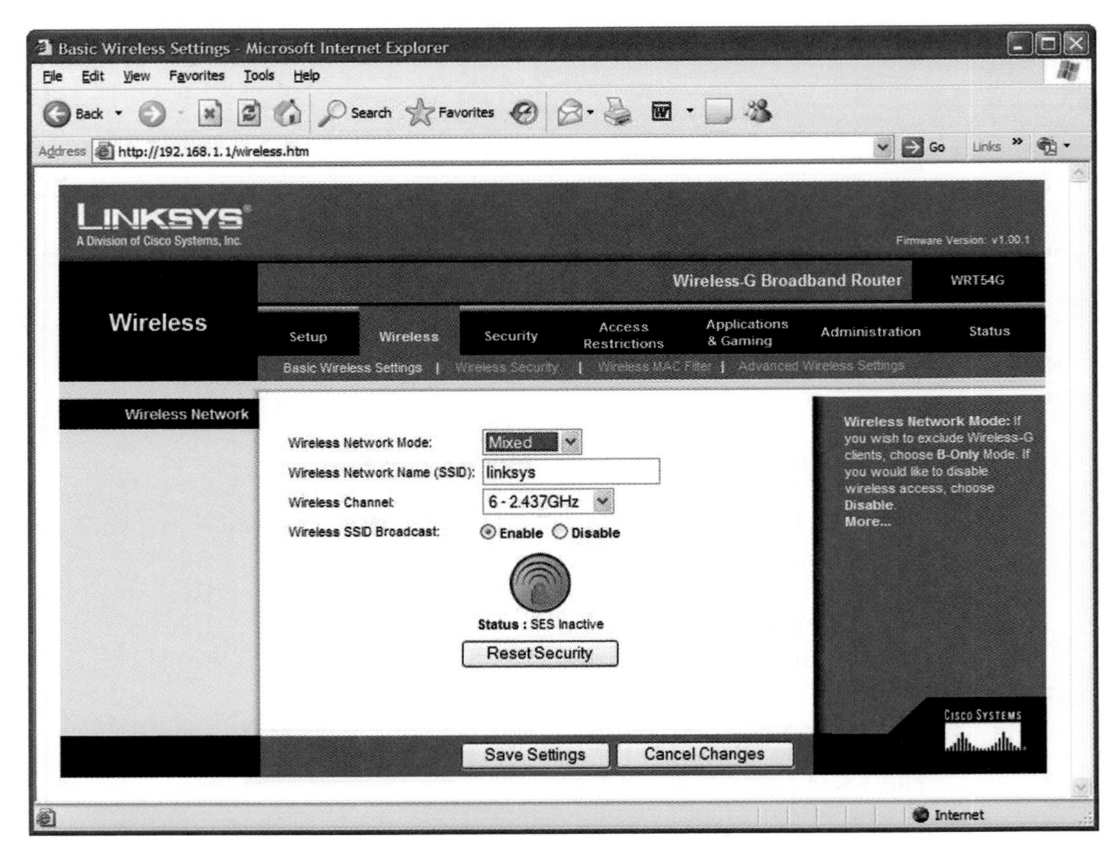

Figure 5-3 Basic Wireless Settings window for a Linksys wireless access point

After you configure the access point, you must help legitimate network users configure their client computers to use the network. In this lab, you practice these tasks.

TROUBLESHOOTING

Answer these questions to set up and configure the wireless access point:

1. What is the IP address of the wireless access point? How did you find the IP address?

   ____

2. Change the password to the wireless access point's setup utility. What is the new password?

   ____

3. If the wireless access point is also a multipurpose router, configure the router to be a firewall so that the router blocks uninvited activity from the Internet. What menu or screen in the router's firmware setup utility did you use to configure the firewall?

   ____

4. Configure the wireless access point to disable SSID broadcasting. What menu or screen did you use?

   ____

5. Configure the wireless access point to filter MAC addresses. What menu or screen did you use?

   ____

6. Configure the wireless access point to encrypt data. What encryption method did you use? What is the encryption passphrase to be used by the client?

   ____

You are ready to configure the wireless client to use this access point. Do the following:

1. Disconnect any network cables or modem cables connected to your wireless computer.
2. Configure the wireless connection using the security features you configured on the access point. List the steps here:

   ____

   ____

   ____

   ____

   ____

   ____

3. Verify that the connection is working by using My Network Places to access the Internet or to copy a file from your computer to another computer on the wireless network.

4. Sometimes a wireless computer automatically connects to the strongest wireless access point it finds, which might mean the computer is connected to an unsecured network that could make you vulnerable to attack. For example, in Figure 5-4, notice the computer is currently connected to an unsecured hot spot. If the user wants to connect to the secured network, she can double-click the secured network listed in the window and then enter a network key to use the network. However, for better security, you can control which access points a computer is allowed to use.

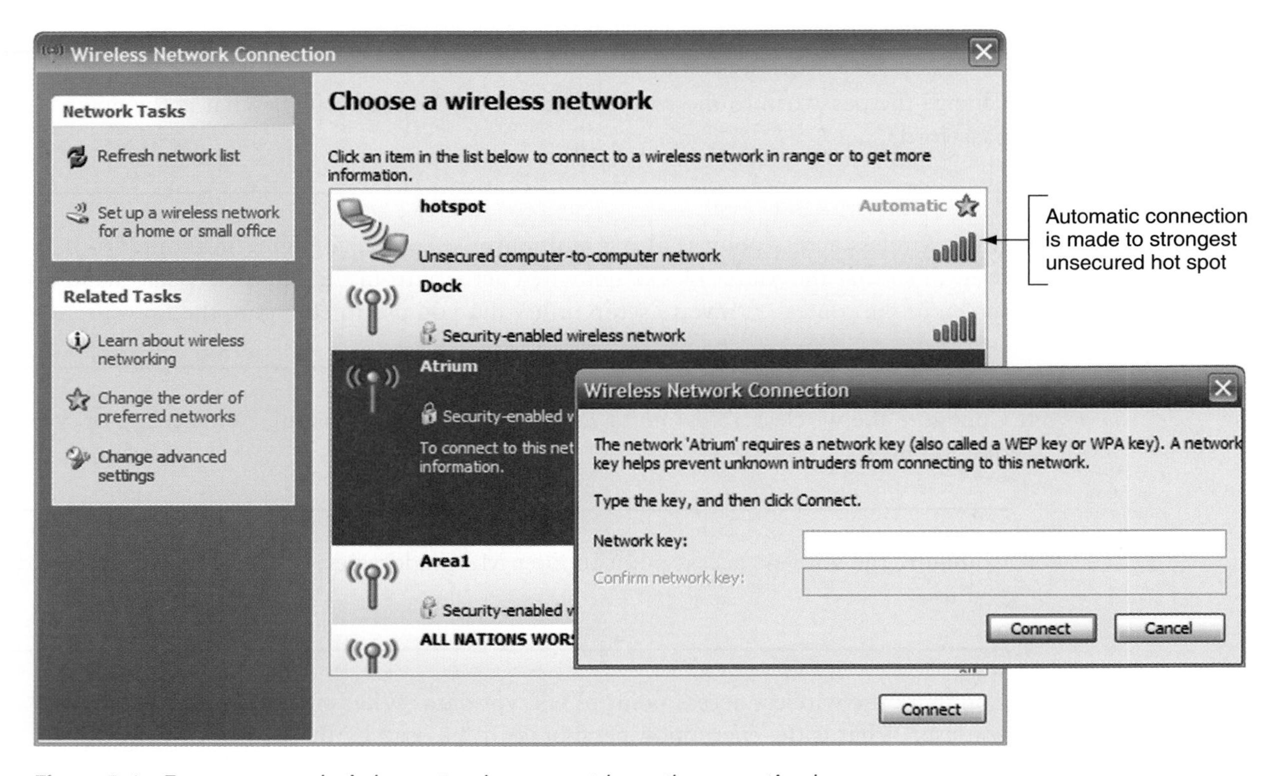

Figure 5-4 To use a secured wireless network, you must know the encryption key

- What is the name of the window in Windows XP that manages the preferred wireless networks for a computer?

  ____

5. Regardless of the wireless network you are using, for the best security, you can block all uninvited communication over the network. List the steps to block any uninvited communication with your computer.

   ____

   ____

   ____

REVIEW QUESTIONS

1. Which encryption method provides better security: WPA, WEP, or WPA2?

   ____

2. Why is it important to change the password to the wireless access point's setup utility?

____

3. Which is faster: 802.11b or 802.11g?

____

4. Does MAC address filtering prevent others from reading data sent over the wireless network?

____

5. If you are using WEP data encryption to secure your wireless network, what information must you give users of the network?

____

6. When using a network that contains both wired and wireless technology, does WPA encryption ensure that data cannot be accessed on the wired portion of the network?

____

SCENARIO 5.3: UNDERSTAND THE OSI MODEL (OPTIONAL)

OBJECTIVES

The goal of this lab is to help you understand some of the concepts and principles of networking technology. After completing this lab, you will be able to:

- Describe the OSI layers.
- Apply the OSI layer principles to networking.

MATERIALS REQUIRED

This lab requires the following:

- Internet access

LAB PREPARATION

Before the lab begins, the instructor or lab assistant needs to do the following:

- Verify that Internet access is available.

SCENARIO BACKGROUND

Network architects use a variety of principles and concepts for communication when designing and implementing networks. Collectively, this architectural model is called the OSI (Open Systems Interconnection) model. The OSI model consists of seven layers. As a PC support technician, you do not need to understand network architecture. However, you might find it interesting to know a little about these fundamental concepts, which can help you better understand how the TCP/IP protocols work.

ESTIMATED COMPLETION TIME: 45 minutes

SCENARIO

Using the Internet for your research, answer the following questions:

1. What are the seven OSI layers? Enter their names in the empty boxes on the left side of Figure 5-5.

OSI Layers			TCP/IP Protocol Stack
7			**Application Layer** (E-mail using SMTP and IMAP protocols)
6			
5			
4			**Transport Layer** (TCP protocol)
3			**Internet Layer** (IP protocol)
2			**Network Layer** (Network card using Ethernet protocol)
1			

Figure 5-5 Describing the OSI model

2. TCP/IP is a suite of protocols that follow the concepts of the OSI model. The four TCP/IP layers are shown on the right side of Figure 5-5. E-mail is one example of a TCP/IP application that works in the Application layer. What are two more examples of applications that work in this layer?

____

____

3. The TCP protocol works at the Transport layer of TCP/IP. Briefly describe the function of the TCP protocol as used in Internet communications.

____

____

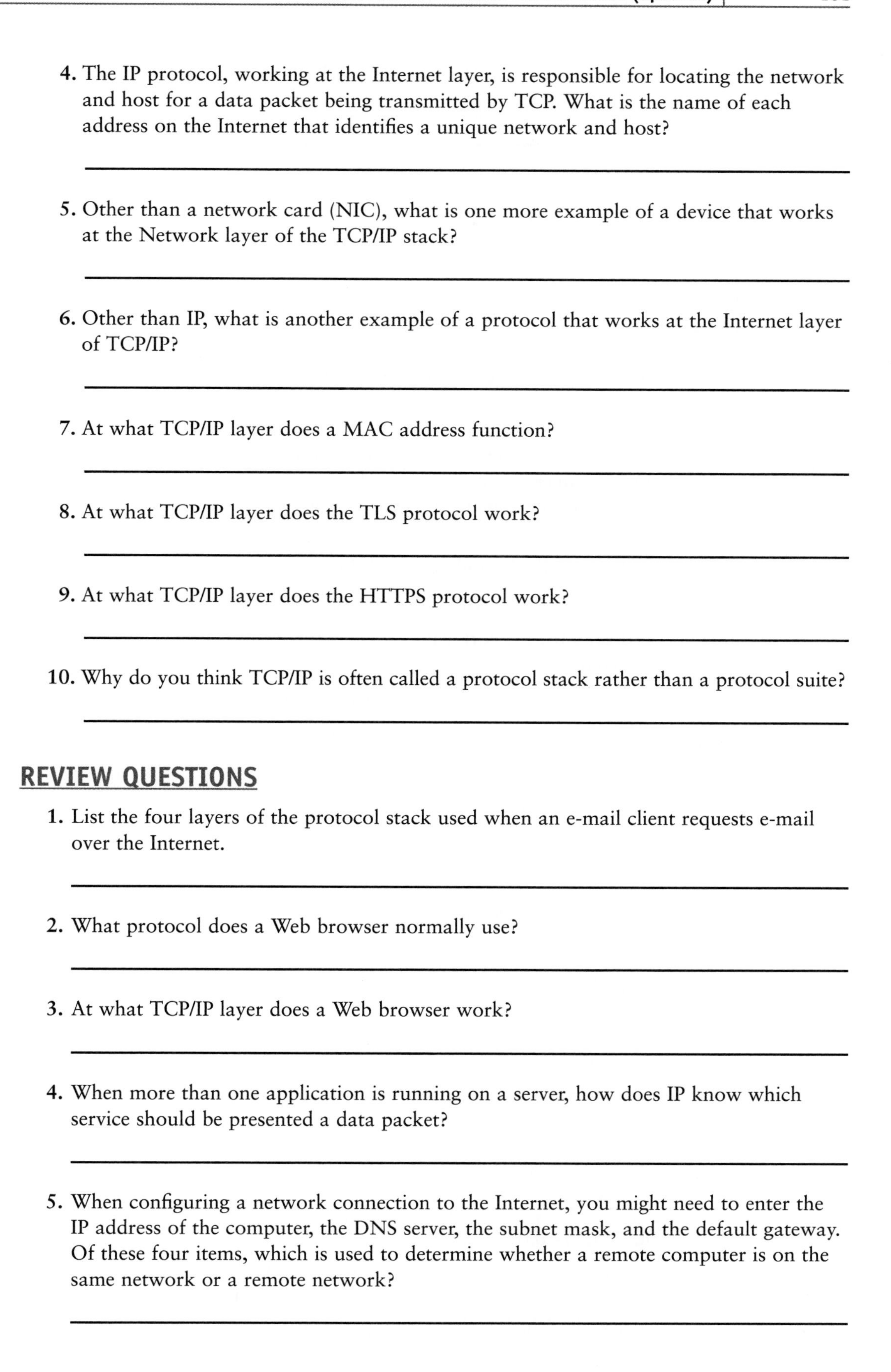

4. The IP protocol, working at the Internet layer, is responsible for locating the network and host for a data packet being transmitted by TCP. What is the name of each address on the Internet that identifies a unique network and host?

____

5. Other than a network card (NIC), what is one more example of a device that works at the Network layer of the TCP/IP stack?

____

6. Other than IP, what is another example of a protocol that works at the Internet layer of TCP/IP?

____

7. At what TCP/IP layer does a MAC address function?

____

8. At what TCP/IP layer does the TLS protocol work?

____

9. At what TCP/IP layer does the HTTPS protocol work?

____

10. Why do you think TCP/IP is often called a protocol stack rather than a protocol suite?

____

REVIEW QUESTIONS

1. List the four layers of the protocol stack used when an e-mail client requests e-mail over the Internet.

____

2. What protocol does a Web browser normally use?

____

3. At what TCP/IP layer does a Web browser work?

____

4. When more than one application is running on a server, how does IP know which service should be presented a data packet?

____

5. When configuring a network connection to the Internet, you might need to enter the IP address of the computer, the DNS server, the subnet mask, and the default gateway. Of these four items, which is used to determine whether a remote computer is on the same network or a remote network?

____

6. Of the four items in Question 5, which is used to relate a domain name to an IP address?

   ____

7. When comparing the IPX/SPX protocol stack to the TCP/IP protocol stack, ______ is to TCP as ______ is to IP.

   ____

PRACTICE EXAM

The following practice exam covers the domain, *Networks*.

1. A network connection in one office of your office building is constantly failing. You notice that the network cable from the centrally located switch to this office passes through an electrical closet. The electrical closet is full of heavy equipment including a central heating unit and a central vacuum unit. Which action is most likely to solve the problem?
   - **a.** Remove the incandescent lighting from the electrical closet and the office
   - **b.** Reroute the network cable around the electrical closet
   - **c.** Install the network cable in a conduit and route the conduit through the walls and ceiling
   - **d.** Install ferrite clamps on the ends of all network cables in the office
2. Which is the fastest network technology?
   - **a.** 802.11g
   - **b.** Fast Ethernet
   - **c.** ISDN
   - **d.** X.25
3. Which of the following is *not* a valid IP address used for networking?
   - **a.** 192.168.0.1
   - **b.** 254.255.0.0
   - **c.** 128.1.1.1
   - **d.** 10.90.13.2
4. Which of the following is a valid subnet mask?
   - **a.** 255.255.255.0
   - **b.** 255.255.10.10
   - **c.** 0.0.0.255
   - **d.** 254.254.0.0
5. Mary has asked you to mount a network drive to the file server, Gorilla. She wants to designate the drive as drive J and point to the folder on the server named Research. Which is the correct path for the drive mount?
   - **a.** \\Gorilla\C:\Research
   - **b.** \\Gorilla\Research

c. /Research/Gorilla

d. //Gorilla/C:/Research

6. You are troubleshooting a network connectivity problem. Which of the following tests can verify that the PC can communicate on the network?

   a. Check the lights on the back of the NIC for activity

   b. Use the Ping command

   c. Look for errors reported about the NIC in Device Manager

   d. Use a loopback port tester to test the network port

7. A computer has been configured for dynamic IP addressing. When you examine the IP address of the computer, you find it to be 169.254.1.10. What is your most likely conclusion?

   a. The computer has been reconfigured to use static IP addressing

   b. The computer network communication is working

   c. The computer cannot connect to the network

   d. The Internet connection is down, but the network connection is working

8. Which of the following network technologies automatically uses encryption?

   a. 802.11g

   b. Bluetooth

   c. USB wireless

   d. Ethernet

9. You are configuring a computer to connect directly to an ISP using a dial-up connection. The ISP has given you a phone number, a user account, and a password, and assures you that no more information is required. What can you assume about the ISP?

   a. The ISP does not use DNS servers

   b. The ISP supports data encryption

   c. The ISP uses the IMAP protocol rather than the POP protocol for e-mail transmissions

   d. The ISP uses dynamic IP addressing

10. When connecting a wireless laptop to an access point, the network administrator asks you for the wireless MAC address of the laptop. What does this tell you about the wireless network?

    a. Data on the wireless network is encrypted for security

    b. Use of the wireless network is limited to certain computers

    c. Data on the wireless network cannot be read by hackers

    d. The wireless network connection is firewalled

11. Which utility is best used to solve problems with the DNS service?

    a. Ping

    b. Tracert

c. Nslookup

d. Ipconfig

12. A company wants to set up a secure Web site to provide private information to its customers. What must happen before the company and its customers can use the HTTPS protocol on the Web site?

    a. The company must purchase a digital certificate

    b. The DNS service must be made aware of the change

    c. The company and each customer must purchase digital certificates

    d. Each customer must download a browser add-on to use the HTTPS protocol

13. Ray brings his laptop to work to connect wirelessly to the local network. He also uses the laptop from public Wi-Fi hot spots. The company network uses static IP addressing, but public hot spots mostly use dynamic IP addressing. What is the best way to configure Ray's laptop so he can connect at all locations?

    a. Set up two hardware profiles, one to connect at work and one to connect in public

    b. Configure TCP/IP for dynamic IP addressing and, on the Alternate Configuration tab, configure the settings for static IP addressing

    c. Configure TCP/IP for static IP addressing and, on the Alternate Configuration tab, configure the settings for dynamic IP addressing

    d. Configure the PC for static IP addressing

14. Jane tells you that her cable modem connection to the Internet is not working. The cable modem is connected to a router, which connects to three PCs on her home network. What do you tell her to do to fix the problem?

    a. Reboot all three PCs. If that does not work, tell her to call her Internet service provider for assistance.

    b. Turn off the cable modem and router. Turn the cable modem back on and wait a few minutes. Then turn the router back on.

    c. Turn off the cable modem and router. Turn the router back on and wait a few minutes. Then turn the cable modem back on.

    d. On each computer on her network, open Device Manager and check for errors reported on the NIC. If no errors are reported, use the Ping command to try to access her ISP.

15. Which command can verify that TCP/IP is installed correctly on a computer?

    a. Ping 127.0.0.1

    b. Ping 127.0.0.0

    c. Ipconfig/all

    d. Nslookup

CHAPTER 6

Security

Troubleshooting scenarios in this chapter:

- **Scenario 6.1**: Audit Computer and Network Activity
- **Scenario 6.2**: Secure a Private Folder

SUMMARY OF DOMAIN CONTENT

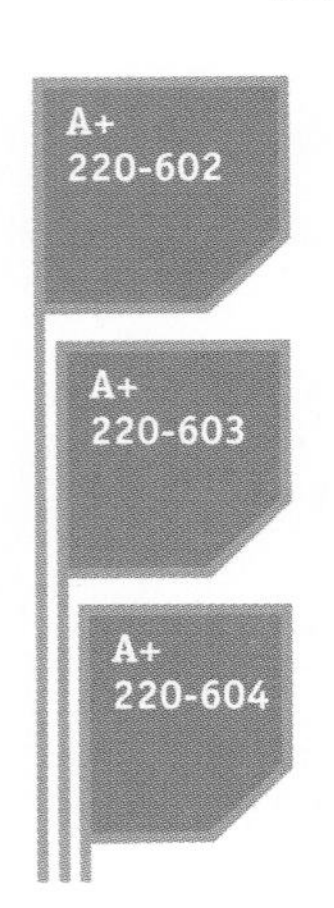

This section of the chapter contains a summary overview of the content in the CompTIA A+ 220-602 Domain 6, *Security*, 220-603 Domain 5, *Security*, and 220-604 Domain 4, *Security*. The high-level objectives for this domain are:

- Identify the fundamentals and principles of security
- Install, configure, upgrade, and optimize security
- Identify tools, diagnostic procedures, and troubleshooting techniques for security (220-602 and 220-603 only)
- Perform preventive maintenance for security (220-602 and 220-603 only)

IDENTIFY THE FUNDAMENTALS AND PRINCIPLES OF SECURITY

Identify the purposes and characteristics of access control. For example:

- ***Access to operating system (e.g., accounts such as user, admin, and guest; groups, permission actions, types, and levels), components, restricted spaces (220-602 and 220-603 only)***
  When Windows 2000/XP is first installed, it automatically creates one administrator account that has full access and one guest account that has strict limitations. User groups are easier to manage than assigning permissions to individual user accounts. Group Policy (gpedit.msc) can be used to secure and control what users can do with a system. A user's available hard drive space can be controlled using disk quotas. Access to storage is controlled using the properties window of a drive, folder, or file. This access can be controlled at the group level or user account level.
- ***Permission levels, types (e.g., file systems and shared), and actions (e.g., read, write, change, and execute) (220-603 only)***
  You share drives, folders, and files using the Sharing tab on the item's properties window. By disabling simple file sharing, you can control which user account or account group can read, write, change, and execute files and folders.
- ***Control access to PCs, servers, laptops, and restricted spaces (applies to hardware and operating systems) (220-604 only)***
  - You can control access to computers using authentication techniques such as user accounts, PINs, smart cards, and biometric data. You can lock down a computer by setting power-on passwords and requiring that all Windows accounts use passwords.
  - Make sure company security polices are clear to all employees. For example, employees should understand that they never leave their desks with sensitive data files left open unless they first lock down their workstations.
  - Never give your passwords to anyone, and make sure company security policies are clear to all employees that they never give out passwords to anyone (including you).
  - To physically secure a system, use computer case locks, chains, and locked rooms.
- ***Identify the purposes and characteristics of auditing and event logging (220-602 only)***
  Some BIOSes offer event logging in which startup errors are recorded. In Windows, you can audit activity using Group Policy and Event Viewer. If simple file sharing

is disabled, you can use the Security tab on the Properties window of a folder or file to audit activity. Monitor network activity using the Windows Firewall window.

INSTALL, CONFIGURE, UPGRADE, AND OPTIMIZE SECURITY

Install and configure software, wireless, and data security. For example:

- *Smart card readers (220-603 and 220-604 only)*
  A smart card reader can use a USB port. It is used to read authentication data stored on a smart card, such as a key fob or a magnetic strip card.
- *Key fobs (220-603 and 220-604 only)*
  A key fob is a type of smart card. Some display a number that changes frequently. A user must enter this number on a logon screen to gain access to a system.
- *Biometric devices (220-603 and 220-604 only)*
  Fingerprint readers and iris scan devices are considered weaker authentication methods than smart cards.
- *Authentication technologies (220-602 and 220-603 only)*
  Authentication proves that you are who you say you are and your identity is validated in a database of authorized accounts. Authentication essentially uses two methods: You prove you are in possession of something (for example, a smart card or biometric data) and you know something (for example, a password). After you are authenticated, permissions assigned to your account control what you can and cannot do on the computer or network. An administrator assigns these permissions based on your job requirements.
- *Software firewalls (220-602 and 220-603 only)*
  Software firewalls include Windows Firewall or third-party software. For stronger protection, use a hardware firewall, such as a router.
- *Auditing and event logging (enable/disable only) (220-602 and 220-603 only)*
  Be familiar with using Group Policy, Event Viewer, the Security tab of a file or folder's Properties window, and CMOS setup to enable and disable event logs.
- *Wireless client configuration (220-602 and 220-603 only)*
  To configure a wireless client to use a secured wireless network, you might need to change the configuration. For example, you can enter the SSID for a hidden network or enable encryption and enter the appropriate passphrase (also called a network key or encryption key). If the secured network is using MAC address filtering, you must tell the network administrator the MAC address.
- *Unused wireless connections (220-602 and 220-603 only)*
  Most laptops have a switch to turn the internal wireless device on and off. For added security, keep the device turned off if you are not using wireless.
- *Data access (e.g., permissions and basic local security policy) (220-602 and 220-603 only)*
  Access to drives, folders, and files is controlled by user accounts and account groups, Group Policy, and the Properties window of the drive, folder, or file.
- *Encryption and encryption technologies (220-603 only)*
  Wi-Fi networks use WEP, WPA, and WPA2 methods for encryption. WPA2 (also known as WPA2-PSK, AES, 802.11i, or 802.11x) is the strongest method. Web browsers, e-mail, and FTP Internet applications can all use HTTPS data encryption methods. The three encryption methods supported by Internet Explorer are SSL (Secure

Sockets Layer), TLS (Transport Layer Security), and PCT (Private Communication Technology). All three methods use digital certificates that validate a company or individual's identity. SSL is the most popular method; an SSL certificate is installed on the server and is bound to the server's static IP address.

- ***File systems (converting from FAT 32 to NTFS only) (220-602 only)***
  By using the Convert.exe program, you can convert a FAT32 volume (also called a logical drive or partition) to use the NTFS file system. For example, to convert drive D to NTFS, use the following command:

  ```
  convert D: /fs:ntfs
  ```

  In Windows, you cannot convert an NTFS volume to FAT32. Also, when installing Windows 2000/XP on a FAT32 drive, the setup process gives you the opportunity to convert the drive to NTFS during the installation.

IDENTIFY TOOLS, DIAGNOSTIC PROCEDURES, AND TROUBLESHOOTING TECHNIQUES FOR SECURITY (220-602 AND 220-603 ONLY)

Diagnose and troubleshoot software and data security issues. For example:

- ***Software firewall issues***
  When Windows Firewall is turned on in Windows XP, you can block all uninvited network activity by checking "Don't allow exceptions" in the Windows Firewall window. Specific exceptions can be allowed for incoming traffic that is not initiated by this computer (for example, to allow Remote Assistance or Remote Desktop to work). On the Advanced tab of the Windows Firewall window, you can enable security logging to monitor network activity. The log file is named pfirewall.log, and is in the Windows folder. For Windows 2000, use third-party firewall software.
- ***Wireless client configuration issues***
  Verify that the SSID is correct, that the correct passphrase is used for encryption, and that the correct encryption method is selected.
- ***Data access issues (e.g., permissions and security policies)***
  When a user cannot access data in a file or folder, consider that the user account might not have permission to use the resource or that the file or folder is not shared correctly on the network. An administrator account has access to all files and folders on a computer.
- ***Encryption and encryption technology issues***
  A user who owns an encrypted file can share it with other users on the same computer by exporting his certificate. Other users can then import the certificate and gain access to the file. Someone with an administrator account can decrypt any encrypted file.

PERFORM PREVENTIVE MAINTENANCE FOR SECURITY (220-602 AND 220-603 ONLY)

Recognize social engineering and address social engineering situations

Social engineering refers to the practice of tricking someone into disclosing private information. E-mail phishing is a common example of social engineering. In an organization, the best defense against social engineering is to create clear company polices about disclosure of information and to make sure employees are familiar with and understand these polices.

SCENARIO 6.1: AUDIT COMPUTER AND NETWORK ACTIVITY

OBJECTIVES

The goal of this lab is to help you learn how to enable event logging in Windows and CMOS setup so that you can audit events as needed to help secure a computer or network. After completing this lab, you will be able to:

- Use Windows tools for event logging.
- Use CMOS setup for event logging.

MATERIALS REQUIRED

This lab requires the following:

- A Windows XP computer connected to a network

LAB PREPARATION

Before the lab begins, the instructor or lab assistant needs to do the following:

- Make a networked Windows XP computer available for each student or workgroup. The computer should not belong to a Windows domain.

SCENARIO BACKGROUND

It is often necessary to monitor or audit computer or network events, such as logon events, failed hardware events, data access events, and other event activity. Auditing is necessary when you are looking for security breaches or troubleshooting hardware or software problems. This lab covers event logging for both of these situations.

ESTIMATED COMPLETION TIME: 1.5 hours

SCENARIO

Samuel works as a PC support technician in a patent attorney's office. The attorneys are especially interested in a high level of security because their clients often trust them with information they are expected to protect. The attorneys know that, in the past, hackers have tried to steal inventions by penetrating the office's computers and networks. Therefore, Samuel wants to implement all available techniques to audit computers that contain client records on the local wired and wireless network.

TROUBLESHOOTING

Samuel has decided he wants to audit events in four areas: network activity, Windows logon, access to private folders, and errors that occur when a computer is booted. All four areas are covered in this lab. Follow these steps to configure your computer for the lab:

1. Create a user account named Attorney Miller. In Miller's My Documents folder, create a folder named Miller_Client_Inventions. If you are using the NTFS file system, any folder that is part of your user profile in the Documents and Settings folder can be

made private using the folder Properties window. For example, to make the folder showing in Figure 6-1 private, check Make this folder private. Make Attorney Miller's My Documents folder private so that other users who are logged on to the computer or the network cannot see this folder. Is the Miller_Client_Inventions folder also private? How do you know?

___

___

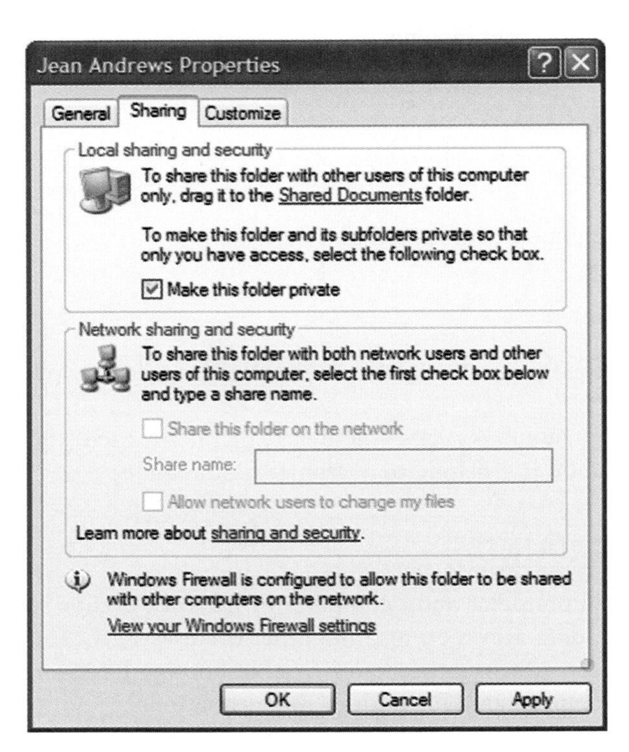

Figure 6-1 A folder that belongs to a user profile can be made private

2. Create a folder named C:\Client_Inventions. Share the folder so that all users have full access to it.
3. Create two document files in the folder. Name the files Smith_Invention and Williams_Invention. Encrypt the contents of the folder. To encrypt a folder, begin by clicking the Advanced button on the General tab of the folder Properties window as showing in Figure 6-2.
4. From another computer on the network, verify that you can see the two files in the Client_Inventions folder. Can you open either file from the remote computer? Why or why not?

___

Follow these steps to audit network activity:

1. Using Windows Firewall, enable security logging. In the Windows Firewall window, under Security Logging, click the Settings button. Logging options are set using the resulting Log Settings dialog box showing in Figure 6-3.

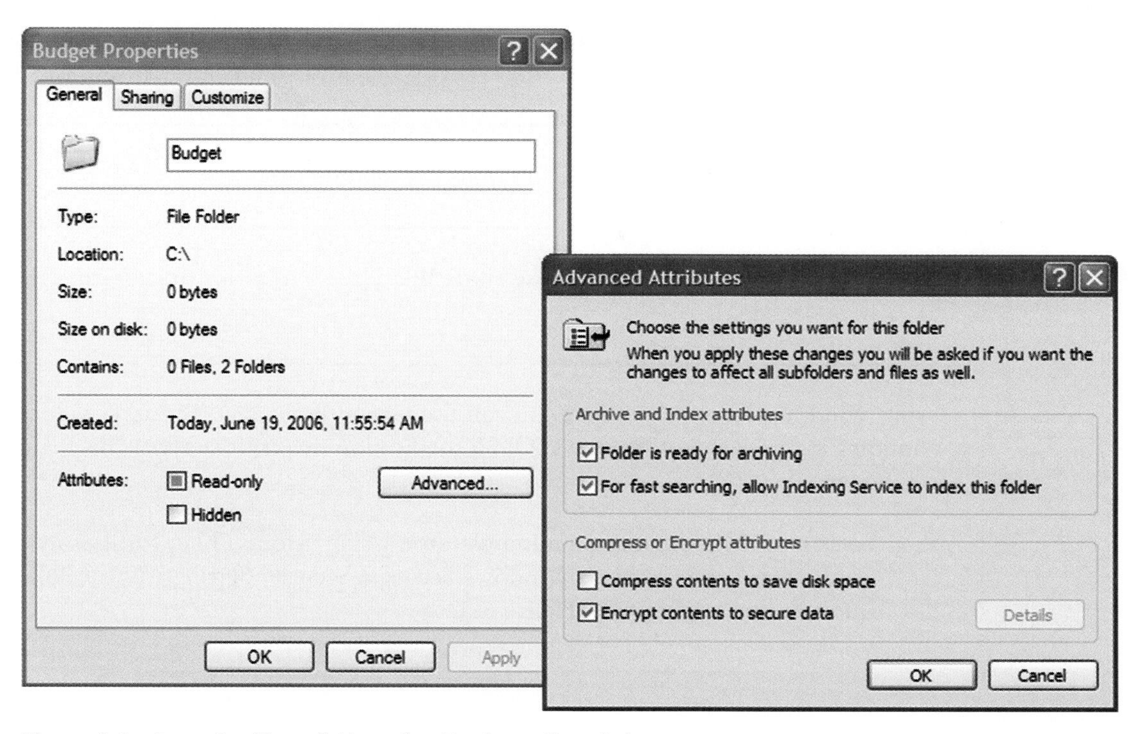

Figure 6-2 Encrypt a file or folder using the Properties window

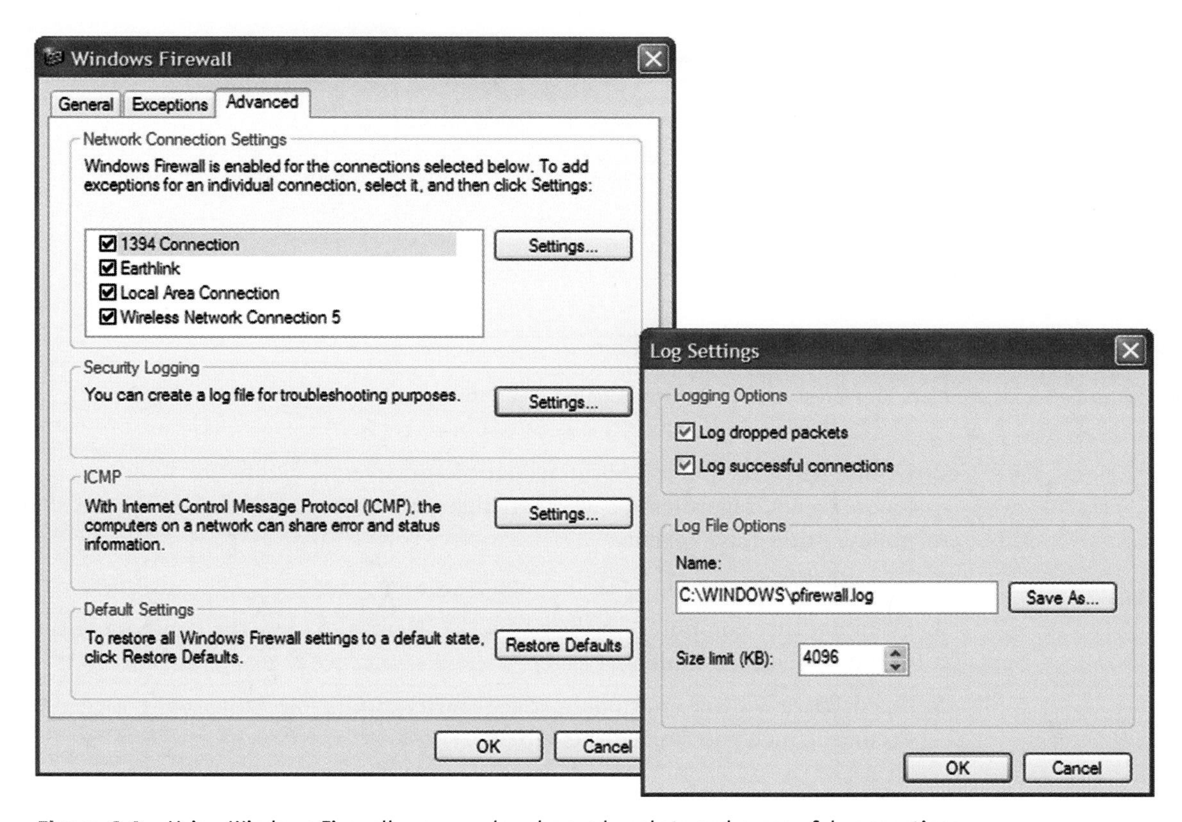

Figure 6-3 Using Windows Firewall, you can log dropped packets and successful connections

2. From another computer on the network, try to access the Client_Inventions folder. Print the log file that shows this event. What is the name and path to the log file?

____

3. In the log file, how is a user or computer identified?

____

4. What is one good reason to use static IP addressing in this office rather than dynamic IP addressing?

____

Using Windows XP Professional, you can use Group Policy and Event Viewer to monitor Windows logon events. (Windows XP Home Edition does not support this feature). Do the following:

1. Log on to the system as an administrator. Using Group Policy, drill down to Computer, Configuration, Windows Settings, Security Settings, Local Policies, and Audit Policy, as shown in Figure 6-4.

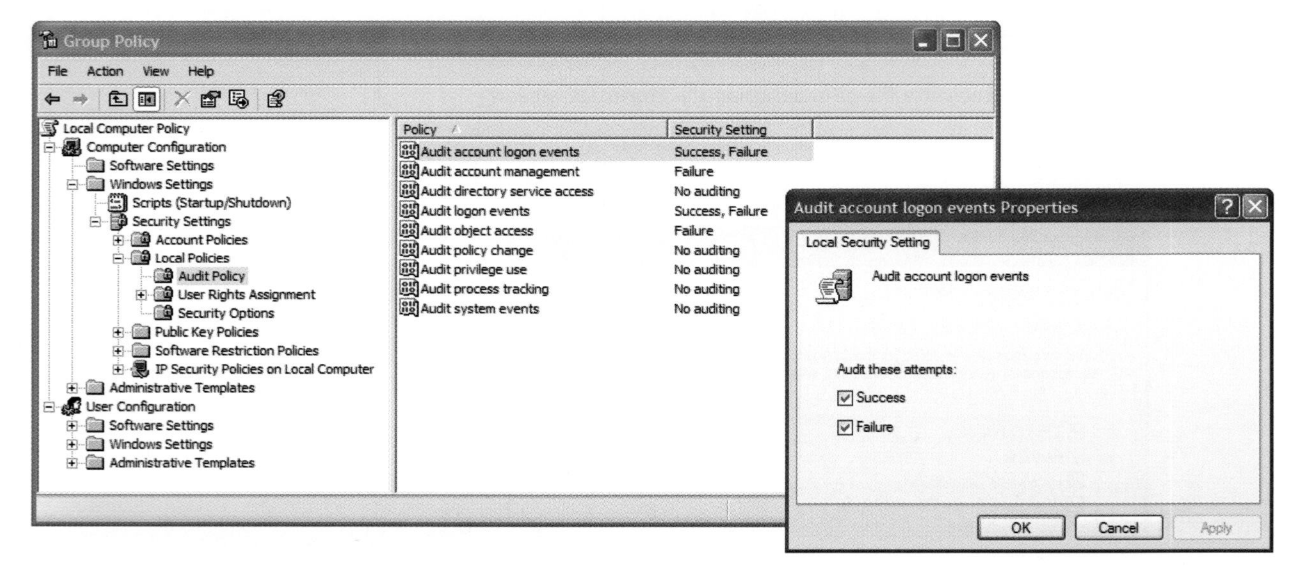

Figure 6-4 Set Windows XP Professional to monitor logging on to the system

2. Double-click the policy, Audit account logon events. Configure Windows to log all logon events, regardless of whether they are successes or failures. Do the same for the policy, Audit logon events.
3. Log off your computer and then log back on.
4. From another computer on the network, attempt to view the contents of the Client_Inventions folder.
5. Open Event Viewer and look at the Security events log. How many logged events have occurred since you started this lab?

____

6. How are remote computers identified in the event log?

____

7. Double-click an event to see detailed information about the event, as shown in Figure 6-5.

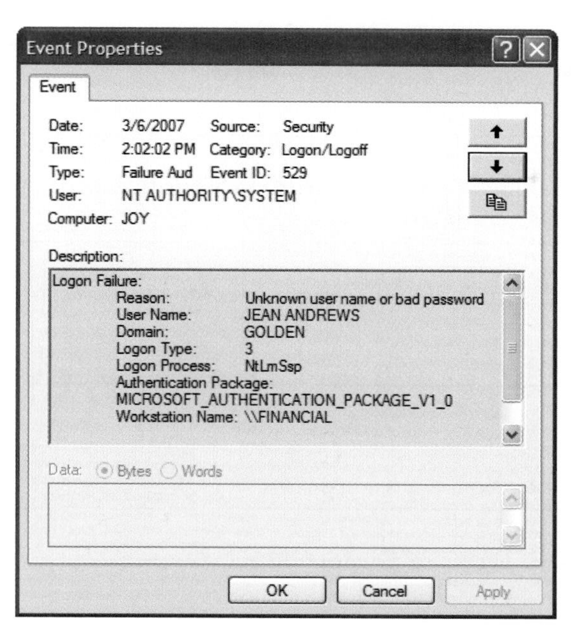

Figure 6-5 Details about a logged event display in the Event Properties dialog box for that event

8. Open the Security Properties window in Event Viewer. Set the Security events log so that events will not be overwritten (see Figure 6-6). Close Event Viewer.

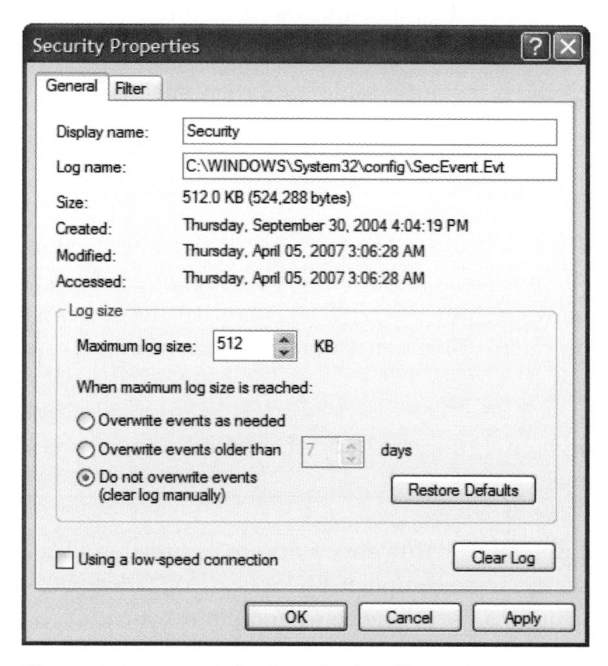

Figure 6-6 Control the Security log file settings

9. Using the Registry Editor, export the HKLM\SYSTEM\CurrentControlSet\Control\Lsa key. Then change the DWORD value of the key to 1, which causes the system to halt if the Security event log fills up. Answer these questions:

- What command did you use to launch the Registry Editor?

____

◢ What menu in the editor did you use to export the Registry key?

____

◢ What did you name the exported key?

____

10. How often do you think you need to clear the Security events log?

____

11. Describe what you must do if you forget to clear the log, which will cause the system to halt.

____

____

____

Do the following to monitor access to private folders:

1. Turn off simple file sharing.
2. Using Group Policy, set the Audit object access policy so that both successes and failures are monitored.
3. Using the Auditing tab of the Advanced Security Settings window for the Client_Inventions folder, configure Windows to monitor the folder for all successful and failed accesses by all users (Everyone).
4. Using Windows Explorer, open the folder and then open a file inside the folder.
5. Open Event Viewer. How many logged events are recorded for this folder?

____

Tip

To lock a workstation without waiting for the screen saver to activate, press Win+L.

When a user walks away from his desk without taking the time to log off Windows, others can use his computer to access private folders. Configure Windows Screen Saver so that the screen saver activates after four minutes of inactivity and, on resume, the user must log on to Windows.

◢ What window did you use to make these changes?

____

Note

To refresh a window in Windows Explorer or Event Viewer, press the F5 key.

In Windows, failed hardware events are recorded in Event Viewer in the System log. However, some computer BIOSes can log failed hardware events during or after startup. Do the following to find out if your BIOS has this ability:

1. Reboot your system and enter CMOS setup.
2. Look on all menus for the ability to record errors during or after startup. Did you find this option? If so, describe exactly what type of error is recorded and how to enable the option:

____

____

To return event logging to the way it was before you started this lab, do the following:

1. Turn off network monitoring.
2. Restore the Group Policy settings so that logon events and object access events are not logged.
3. Restore the Registry key you changed by double-clicking the exported key file. Then delete the exported file.
4. Remove all auditing from the Client_Inventions folder.
5. Turn on simple file sharing.

In conclusion, answer the following questions. You might find it interesting to discuss your answers with others in this lab.

1. Sometimes, too much information keeps you from effectively monitoring a system. In this lab you have monitored many types of failed and successful events, which all generate a lot of data to plow through. How do you think Samuel could improve the monitoring methods and options used in this lab?

   ____

   ____

   ____

2. The current network is configured as a Windows workgroup. Give two reasons Samuel should recommend that the attorneys convert the network to a Windows domain.

   ____

   ____

   ____

   ____

REVIEW QUESTIONS

1. What is the name of the Windows Firewall log file that monitors network activity?

   ____

2. What happens when the allowable size of the log file that monitors network activity has been exceeded?

   ____

3. Which applet in Control Panel is used to turn simple file sharing on and off?

   ____

4. What is the name of the Group Policy console program file?

____

5. What are the two main categories of policies in the Group Policy console?

____

SCENARIO 6.2: SECURE A PRIVATE FOLDER

OBJECTIVES

The goal of this lab is to help you learn how to apply Windows tools to secure a private folder. After completing this lab, you will be able to:

- Share a folder on the network.
- Control which users can read or modify the folder.

MATERIALS REQUIRED

This lab requires the following:

- Two Windows XP computers connected on a network for each workgroup of two or more students

LAB PREPARATION

Before the lab begins, the instructor or lab assistant needs to do the following:

- Make a networked Windows XP computer available for each student or student workgroup.

SCENARIO BACKGROUND

In an office environment, employees often share files and folders as they work together on a common project. Sensitive information in these shared files and folders often needs to be kept private from others in the organization. A PC support technician will probably be asked to solve these types of security issues for the office. In this lab, you learn how to apply Windows security tools and features to solve these security problems.

ESTIMATED COMPLETION TIME: 1 hour

SCENARIO

Michael is team leader of the payroll department of Peaceful Arbor, Inc., a corporation that manages assisted living facilities. He and his two other team members, Sharon and Jason, share payroll files that others in the accounting department are not allowed to view. The payroll data is stored on the file server in the C:\Payroll folder, and everyone in the accounting department who is not on the payroll team knows not to open the folder. Recently, Michael suspects that others have been poking around where they don't belong, so he has turned to Linden, the PC support technician, for help.

TROUBLESHOOTING

Working with a team member, recreate the problem on your two networked lab computers by doing the following:

1. On Computer 1, which will be your file server, create a user account named Linden and assign administrative privileges to the account. Be sure to assign a password to this account. What is the password?

   ---

2. On Computer 1, create the folder C:\Payroll. Create three spreadsheet files named MasterPayroll.xls, October2007.xls, and November2007.xls. Put some bogus data in each file, and store all three files in the C:\Payroll folder.
3. On Computer 1, create the folder C:\Budget. Create two spreadsheet files named Budget2007.xls and Budget2008.xls. Put some bogus data in each file, and store the files in the C:\Budget folder.
4. Configure Computer 2 so that passwords of at least six characters are required for all user accounts. To do this, use the policy Minimum password length, shown in Figure 6-7.

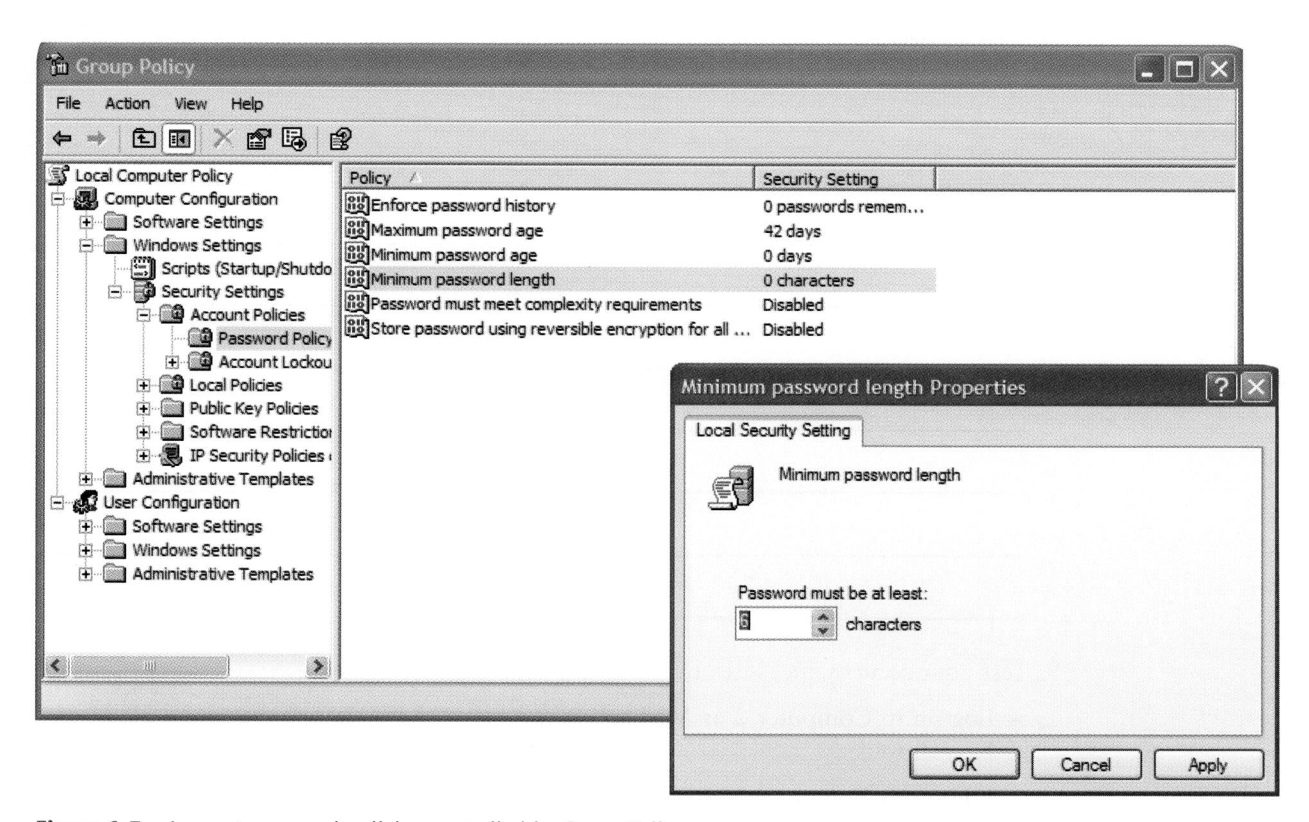

Figure 6-7 Account password policies controlled by Group Policy

5. On Computer 2, create a limited user account named Michael. Michael belongs to the payroll team and needs full access to the Payroll folder. He also needs access to the Budget folder. What is the password to the Michael account?

____

6. On Computer 2, create a limited user account named Sharon. Sharon belongs to the payroll team and needs full access to the Payroll folder. She does not need any access to the Budget folder. What is the password to the Sharon account?

____

7. Create a limited user account named Jason on Computer 2. Jason belongs to the accounting department and needs full access to the Budget folder, but should not have any access to the Payroll folder. What is the password to the Jason account?

____

8. Using Windows tools, set the permissions and access controls so that Michael, Sharon, and Jason can read and write to the folder they need, but cannot view the contents of the folder they are not allowed to see. List the steps you took to do the job:

____

____

____

____

____

____

____

____

____

____

9. Test your security measures by doing the following:
   - Log on to Computer 2 as Michael. Edit a file in the Budget folder and a file in the Payroll folder.
   - Log on to Computer 2 as Sharon. Edit a file in the Payroll folder.
   - Verify that Sharon cannot view the contents of the Budget folder.
   - Log on to Computer 2 as Jason. Edit a file in the Budget folder.
   - Verify that Jason cannot view the contents of the Payroll folder.

10. When you are convinced you have solved the problem, do the following to further test your system:

   - Ask someone on another team to try to hack through your security measures using Computer 2. Was this person able to break through? If so, how?

     ____

     ____

   - Ask the same person to attempt to hack through your security measures using Computer 1. Was this person able to break through? If so, how?

     ____

     ____

11. Correct any security problems that have come to light by your testing. What, if anything, did you need to do?

   ____

   ____

   ____

   ____

12. Set up event logging so that you can view a log of unauthorized attempts to view a folder. How did you do it?

   ____

   ____

   ____

   ____

   ____

13. Test your auditing method by logging on to Computer 2 as Jason and attempting to view the Payroll folder. Print the screen that shows the logged event.

REVIEW QUESTIONS

1. What window can you use to disable simple file sharing?

   ____

2. What is the extension of the exported file created when you export a certificate?

   ____

3. What utility is used to require that each user account must have a password?

   ____

4. Why is it important for people besides your own team to test a security system that your team has put in place?

____

5. There is often more than one way to solve a problem. Check with another team that completed this lab and see how it accomplished the tasks. Were there any differences between their methods and yours?

____

PRACTICE EXAM

The following practice exam covers the domain, *Security*.

1. Before you can view the Security log in Windows XP Event Viewer, you must:
   a. Install Windows XP Service Pack 2
   b. Log in as an administrator
   c. Use Group Policy to activate security logging
   d. Use Event Viewer to turn on security logging
2. How do you access the Group Policy window?
   a. Control Panel -> Administrative Tools -> Group Policy
   b. Control Panel -> Administrative Tools -> Computer Management -> Group Policy
   c. Enter gpedit.msc in the Run dialog box
   d. Either b or c
3. Mary's user account belongs to the Accountant user group, which is assigned Full Control to a folder. Her account also belongs to the Business group, which has Read permission to the same folder. Which is true when she accesses the folder?
   a. Mary can read, edit, and delete files in the folder
   b. Mary can read and edit files in the folder, but cannot delete them
   c. Mary can only read, but cannot edit or delete files in the folder
   d. Mary can modify files in the folder
4. What is required to enable the Security tab on a folder's Properties window?
   a. Use the NTFS file system
   b. Under Folder Options, uncheck simple file sharing
   c. Use Windows XP Professional rather than Windows XP Home Edition
   d. All of the above
5. Jason is called to the payroll department to help fix a scanner problem. While he is there, he notices that an employee has left her desk leaving the payroll database open on her screen. What should he do?
   a. Fix the scanner problem and say nothing about the open database
   b. Tell the employee's boss what he has observed and recommend he tell the employee to close data files when she leaves her desk

c. Recommend to the department boss that he send a memorandum to all employees about closing data files before they leave their desk

d. Log the employee off her workstation

e. Close the payroll database

6. Which security feature helps assure that a workstation gets locked down when a user leaves his desk?

a. Check *On resume, display Welcome screen* in the Display Properties window

b. Require a supervisor password to the CMOS setup utility

c. Use a lock and chain to secure a laptop computer to a desk

d. Turn off simple file sharing

7. A supervisor complains that files in a shared folder have been tampered with by employees who use the company's wireless network that are not authorized to access this folder. What is the best way to fix the problem? (Choose two answers.)

a. Do not share this folder on the network

b. Turn off simple file sharing and set permission for the folder so that only authorized users can view and modify the folder

c. Use better security for the wireless network including MAC address filtering and data encryption

d. Encrypt the folder and its subfolders and then share the certificate used to encrypt the folder with others who need access to the folder

8. What tool can be used to require that Windows user account passwords be changed every 30 days?

a. The User Accounts applet in Control Panel

b. The Administrative Tools applet in Control Panel

c. The Display Properties window

d. Group Policy

9. Which authentication technique provides the strongest security?

a. Require a six-character password and a smart card scan

b. Collect two scans of biometric data: an iris scan and a fingerprint scan

c. Require a password that is at least eight characters long and includes numbers, letters, and symbols

d. Use a smart card to gain access to a computer or network

10. Ned wants to know whenever someone in his office uses the local network to access his computer. What tool does he use?

a. Group Policy console

b. Windows Firewall

c. Services console

d. System Monitor

11. Which of the following methods provides the best security for data sent over a wireless network?
    a. MAC address filtering
    b. WPA encryption
    c. WEP encryption
    d. An SSL certificate
12. What tool or command do you use to change a FAT32 volume to an NTFS volume?
    a. Disk Management
    b. Diskpart
    c. Sysprep
    d. Convert
13. James has a desktop computer at work that holds valuable data he must access from home and on the road. You have been asked to configure the network and desktop to serve up Remote Desktop for his use. What do you need to do to configure the network?
    a. Verify the company uses static IP addressing for Internet access and configure the router for port forwarding
    b. Use dynamic IP addressing on the router and use static IP addressing on the desktop
    c. Disable Windows Firewall on the desktop and turn off the firewall feature on the router
    d. Run the Remote Desktop wizard, which will configure both the desktop and the network
14. Your supervisor calls you to say he needs to check Event Viewer on the local file server and needs the password to your account, which has administrative permissions on the server. What do you do?
    a. Give your supervisor the password
    b. Do not give the password and site company policy as your reason
    c. Tell your boss you cannot give him your password, but offer to log on to the file server and sit with your boss while he reads the event logs
    d. Write the password on a sticky note and put it on the file server for easy access
15. You suspect a customer's computer is infected with a virus. Antivirus software is already installed on the computer. What should you do before you run the AV scan?
    a. Verify the AV software is not pirated
    b. Update the AV software with the latest virus definitions
    c. Close all open applications
    d. Log on to Windows as an administrator

CHAPTER 7

Safety and Environmental Issues

Troubleshooting scenarios in this chapter:

- **Scenario 7.1**: Learn about Safety Issues
- **Scenario 7.2**: Safely Clean Computer Equipment

SUMMARY OF DOMAIN CONTENT

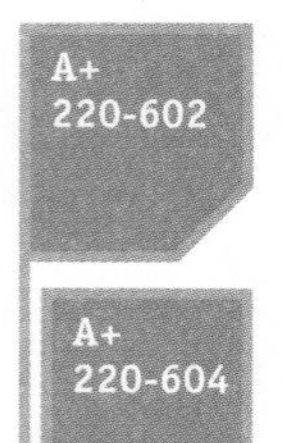

This section of the chapter contains a summary overview of the content in the CompTIA A+ 220–602 Domain 7, *Safety and Environmental Issues* and 220–604 Domain 5, *Safety and Environmental Issues*. Please note that the 220–603 exam does not include the *Safety and Environmental Issues* domain. The high-level objective for this domain is:

- Identify potential hazards and proper safety procedures, including power supply, display devices, and environment (e.g., trip, liquid, situational, and atmospheric hazards, and high-voltage and moving equipment)

IDENTIFY POTENTIAL HAZARDS AND PROPER SAFETY PROCEDURES, INCLUDING POWER SUPPLY, DISPLAY DEVICES, AND ENVIRONMENT (E.G., TRIP, LIQUID, SITUATIONAL, AND ATMOSPHERIC HAZARDS, AND HIGH-VOLTAGE AND MOVING EQUIPMENT)

- Manufacturers of cleaning solutions and pads provide a material safety data sheet (MSDS) that explains how to properly handle and store chemical solvents. The MSDS also includes information about health and first aid for the product. Keep the MSDS on hand in your lab or office. If you have an accident with chemicals, your organization might require you to fill out an incident report.
- To protect a system against ESD (static electricity) when you work inside the case or with sensitive computer components, wear a ground bracelet or use a ground mat, static shielding bags, or antistatic gloves. Don't ground yourself when working inside CRT monitors, laser printers, or power supplies. Protect expansion cards, memory modules, and drives against ESD by storing them in antistatic bags.
- A Class C fire extinguisher is rated to put out fires fueled by electricity.
- Keep water away from electrical equipment including computers. Don't turn on or service a computer in a wet area.
- When shipping a computer, first remove any discs and tapes from their drives, back up the hard drive, and disconnect all peripherals. Pack the monitor, case, and other devices in their original shipping cartons or similar boxes.
- Dispose of used equipment according to local government regulations. This equipment includes batteries, battery packs, toner cartridges, power supplies, monitors, cases, and chemical solvents.
- Some laser printers produce ozone and contain an ozone filter to protect the atmosphere. For these printers, replace the filter when recommended by the printer manufacturer.

SCENARIO 7.1: LEARN ABOUT SAFETY ISSUES

OBJECTIVES

The goal of this lab is to help you learn about safety issues while working on computers and repairing them. After completing this lab, you will be able to:

- Describe safety concerns of computer users.
- Describe how to protect yourself and the equipment as you repair a computer.

MATERIALS REQUIRED

- No equipment is necessary.

LAB PREPARATION

- No lab preparation is necessary.

SCENARIO BACKGROUND

A PC support technician is expected to know how to support computer users and keep the computers in good repair. Part of that support includes knowing about safety and environmental issues and making users aware of these issues. This lab covers such concerns.

SCENARIO

Working at a computer for hours on end can be dangerous to your health! I remember sitting around a lunch table with coworkers one day as we shared stories about our strained eyes, wrists, backs, and shoulders, resulting from hours in front of a computer. Suddenly, it dawned on us all that we had better learn how to protect ourselves from this hazardous vocation. Here are some useful tips:

- To prevent carpal tunnel syndrome, keep your wrists straight and your elbows about even with your keyboard. Occasionally stop, relax, and flex your hands, wrists, and arms.
- If you must talk on the phone as you work, you can prevent neck and back strain by using a headset that frees your hands from the phone and keeps you from having to tilt your head to the side.
- To protect your mental health and keep a positive and friendly attitude, don't face the wall as you work. Turn your desk toward a window or toward the center of the room.
- To help prevent eyestrain as you work, occasionally look away from your monitor, focusing on something in the distance and blinking your eyes rapidly. (People who stare at a monitor blink less often than normal, which can dry out their eyes.)
- Keep your head and neck upright and in line with your torso, not bent down or bent backward.
- Keep your torso upright, not bending down. Avoid hunching over your keyboard.
- Draw your keyboard close enough to your body that you don't need to extend your arms outward. Keep your elbows close to your body.
- Your chair needs support for your back (lumbar area). The seat should be comfortable, with rounded edges for your knees.
- Position your monitor directly in front of you, not to the left or right, and not so high or low that you have to bend your head or neck.
- If you are working for long hours at a computer, use a desktop rather than a laptop. A laptop screen is too close to the keyboard for comfort. If you must use a laptop, also use an external keyboard and/or monitor.
- Take breaks! Every 30 to 60 minutes, stand up, walk about, and get a drink. Every one to two hours, do some light exercise such as stretching and bending.

A PC support technician needs to know how to protect himself and the equipment as he works. Here are some useful tips:

- Use a ground bracelet. Attach the bracelet to any grounded surface. If you attach it to the computer case, all static electricity between you and the case will dissipate. You can then work safely inside the case. For added protection, use a ground mat.
- To protect yourself when working inside devices that contain highly charged capacitors, don't ground yourself. Such devices include laser printers, power supplies, and CRT monitors.

Note

You should not work inside a CRT monitor or power supply unless you understand the circuitry inside them. Working inside these devices is not considered an A+ skill for A+ repair technicians. There are no field replaceable units inside these devices.

- As you work on computer hardware, keep a Class C fire extinguisher close by your workbench.

REVIEW QUESTIONS

1. If you use a chemical solvent in your lab, what document should you keep on hand that describes the solvent's health effects, first aid, proper handling, and storage procedures?

   ____

2. A user complains that his computer crashes at odd times. After asking some questions, you find out the user's office is very hot. What is the likely cause of the problem?

   ____

3. Why is it best not to use a laptop computer for long hours of work?

   ____

4. When working inside a CRT monitor, why is it important not to wear a ground bracelet?

   ____

5. How can a user prevent eyestrain when using a monitor for a long time?

   ____

SCENARIO 7.2: SAFELY CLEAN COMPUTER EQUIPMENT

OBJECTIVES

The goal of this lab is to help you learn about safety issues while cleaning and maintaining computers. After completing this lab, you will be able to:

- Clean a computer and other computer parts without damage to yourself or the computer.

MATERIALS REQUIRED

This lab requires the following:

- Computer designed for this lab
- Can of compressed air and/or antistatic vacuum
- Contact cleaner
- Cotton swab
- Isopropyl alcohol (not rubbing alcohol) or liquid soap
- Sticky tape or duct tape
- Soft cloth or antistatic monitor wipes
- ESD bracelet
- Plastic cable ties

LAB PREPARATION

Before the lab begins, the instructor or lab assistant needs to do the following:

- Verify that a computer is available for each student or workgroup.
- Verify cleaning materials listed above are available. These items can be shared among workgroups.

 Note

In this lab, students clean a computer. The instructor might consider taking the students to an office or computer lab on campus where computers are in need of cleaning.

SCENARIO BACKGROUND

A PC support technician is expected to know how to maintain a computer and its peripherals. You need to know how to clean a monitor, mouse, keyboard, and computer system without damaging the equipment or yourself. This lab covers such concerns.

SCENARIO

Table 7-1 lists guidelines to maintain and clean computer equipment.
Following the guidelines in Table 7-1, do the following to clean a computer:

1. Shut down the computer and unplug it.
2. Clean the keyboard, monitor, and mouse.

Component	Cleaning and Maintenance	How Often
Keyboard	**◢ Turn the keyboard upside down and lightly bump keys to dislodge dirt, food, and trash.** **◢ Use a damp cloth to clean the surface.** **◢ Use compressed air or an antistatic vacuum to blow out dust and dirt.** **◢ If a few keys don't work, remove the key caps and spray contact cleaner into the key well. Repeatedly depress the contact to clean it.**	**Monthly**

Table 7-1 Guidelines for cleaning computer equipment

Mouse	◢ To clean a mechanical mouse, first remove the cover of the mouse ball from the bottom of the mouse. ◢ Use compressed air to blow out the ball cavity. ◢ Clean the rollers with a cotton swab dipped in a very small amount of liquid soap or isopropyl alcohol (not rubbing alcohol). For really dirty rollers, use a toothpick or end of a paper clip to pick dirt off the rollers. ◢ Use sticky tape to clean the mouse ball.	Monthly
Monitor	◢ Make sure monitor vents are not obstructed. ◢ If the vents look clogged with dust, use a vacuum to suck out the dust. (Don't open the monitor case.) ◢ Clean the outside of the monitor case with a damp cloth. ◢ Clean the screen with a soft dry cloth. For especially dirty screens, use antistatic monitor wipes which contain a small amount of isopropyl alcohol and are safe for laptop LCD screens.	At least monthly
Inside the case	◢ Make sure the computer case is sitting in a location where air vents are not obstructed and the case will not be kicked. ◢ Use compressed air to blow the dust out of the case, or use an antistatic vacuum to clean vents, power supply, and fans. Be sure all fans and vents are dust free. ◢ Ensure that memory modules and expansion cards are firmly seated. ◢ Use plastic cable ties to tie cables out of the way of airflow. ◢ Be sure all empty bays and empty expansion slots have faceplates installed.	Yearly or whenever you open the case for repairs or installations
Written records of hardware maintenance	◢ Keep an MSDS on file for each chemical you use in your computer lab. ◢ Record when and what preventive maintenance is performed. Record any repairs done to the PC.	Whenever changes are made

Table 7-1 Guidelines for cleaning computer equipment (continued)

3. Clean the outside of the computer case.
4. Open the computer case. Connect the ESD bracelet to the side of the computer case as shown in Figure 7-1. Be sure to connect the clip to case metal, not plastic.
5. Clean the dust from inside the case. Verify case fans can turn freely.
6. Verify that cables are out of the way of airflow. Use cable ties as necessary.
7. Check that each expansion card and memory module is securely seated in its slot. Remove and reseat the card or memory module as needed.
8. Close the case and plug in the power cord.
9. Power up the system and verify that all is working.
10. Clean up around your work area. If you left dust on the floor as you blew it out of the computer case, be sure to clean it up.

Figure 7-1 An ESD bracelet, which protects computer components against ESD, can clip to the side of the computer case and eliminate ESD between you and the case

REVIEW QUESTIONS

1. Why is it necessary to use an ESD bracelet when you work inside a computer case?

   ____

2. Why is it necessary to have an MSDS on file in a computer lab?

   ____

3. Why should monitor vents not be obstructed?

   ____

4. Why is it important that computer fans not be clogged with dust?

   ____

5. What is the purpose of installing faceplates on empty bays and expansion slots?

   ____

PRACTICE EXAM

The following practice exam covers the domain, *Safety and Environmental Issues*.

1. Which chemical can safely be used when cleaning a monitor screen?
   a. Rubbing alcohol
   b. Isopropyl alcohol
   c. Liquid soap
   d. No chemicals should be used on a monitor screen; only use a dry cloth
2. When packing a computer for shipping, which of the following protects the computer equipment from damage?
   a. Back up all important data on the hard drive
   b. Remove a CD or DVD from the optical drive
   c. Unplug all power cords and cables and securely tie them
   d. Both b and c
   e. All of the above
3. What is the purpose of connecting an ESD bracelet to your arm and to the side of the computer case?
   a. To ground the computer case
   b. To ground yourself
   c. To eliminate static electricity in the air
   d. To eliminate static electricity between you and the case
4. A multimeter shows zero resistance when measuring resistance on a fuse. What can you conclude?
   a. The fuse is bad and needs replacing
   b. The fuse is good
   c. The multimeter is not set correctly to test the fuse
   d. The multimeter is not functioning correctly and needs replacing
5. A user complains that her optical mouse is not working as well as it has in the past, causing the curser to move slowly or with jerks on the screen. What do you do to fix the problem?
   a. Clean the rollers and ball inside the mouse
   b. Update the mouse drivers
   c. Download current Windows updates to this system
   d. Check that the mouse is not sitting on glass or a similar shiny surface
6. What do you do when a chemical has been spilled in your computer lab?
   a. Call 911
   b. Use a Class C fire extinguisher to blow chemicals over the spill
   c. Consult the MSDS for this product
   d. Consult the MSDT for this product

7. When you connect the clip on an ESD bracelet to the computer case, why is it important to connect the clip to metal and not plastic?
   a. Because plastic is not a good conductor
   b. Because metal is not a good conductor
   c. Because static electricity does not affect metal
   d. Because computer cases do not contain plastic parts
8. Your supervisor tells you to discard several boxes of computer parts. In one box you find a power supply, a laptop battery, and a printer toner cartridge. What do you do?
   a. Tape the box up tightly and put it in the garbage bin at the back of your office building
   b. Return the toner cartridge to the manufacturer. Call your recycle center to see if it will accept the power supply and battery.
   c. Check the Web site of each device manufacturer for disposal instructions
   d. Vacuum out the inside of the power supply and toner cartridge and then put all parts in the trash
9. Which action is beyond the scope of a PC repair technician trained to receive A+ certification?
   a. Work inside a power supply
   b. Clean the inside of a computer case
   c. Clean spilled toner, dust, and paper particles from a laser printer
   d. Replace a faulty motherboard
10. What is the best tool to use to clean paper and dust from the inside of a laser printer?
    a. Can of compressed air
    b. Soft dry cloth
    c. Soft cloth dampened with alcohol
    d. Soft damp cloth
11. Which device should be stored in an antistatic bag when it is not being used?
    a. Network card
    b. Network cable
    c. Router
    d. Mouse
12. Which type fire extinguisher should you keep in your computer repair lab?
    a. Class A fire extinguisher
    b. Class B fire extinguisher
    c. Class C fire extinguisher
    d. Class D fire extinguisher

13. While working in a customer's office, you notice the computer case is sitting under his desk near his feet. What should you do?
    a. Turn the computer over on its side so it is less likely to be kicked over
    b. Recommend to the customer he wrap padding around the case to protect it from being kicked
    c. Say nothing. Computer cases are tough and can stand an occasional kick.
    d. Recommend to the customer he move the case to a safer location
14. Maria complains her monitor is making strange whining noises. When you arrive at her workstation, you notice stacks of magazines on both sides of the monitor case. What do you do?
    a. Move the magazines so the monitor vents are not obstructed and use an antistatic vacuum to clean the vents
    b. Exchange her CRT monitor for an LCD monitor
    c. Reinstall the video adapter drivers
    d. Install a UPS device between the monitor and the electrical outlet
15. What is the first thing you should do before you clean the dust from inside a computer case?
    a. Unplug the computer from its power source
    b. Disconnect the video cable from the computer
    c. Make sure all case fans can freely turn
    d. Shut down the computer

CHAPTER

8

Communication and Professionalism

Troubleshooting scenarios in this chapter:

- **Scenario 8.1:** Practice Help Desk Skills
- **Scenario 8.2:** Practice Skills for Good Communication

SUMMARY OF DOMAIN CONTENT

This section of the chapter contains a summary overview of the content in the CompTIA A+ 220-602 Domain 8, *Communication and Professionalism* and 220-603 Domain 6, *Communication and Professionalism*. Please note the 220-604 exam does not include the *Communication and Professionalism* domain. The high-level objectives for this domain are:

- Use good communication skills, including listening and tact/discretion, when communicating with customers and colleagues
- Use job-related professional behavior including notation of privacy, confidentiality, and respect for the customer and customers' property

USE GOOD COMMUNICATION SKILLS, INCLUDING LISTENING AND TACT/DISCRETION, WHEN COMMUNICATING WITH CUSTOMERS AND COLLEAGUES

Use clear, concise, and direct statements

- Stay focused on the problem at hand; don't allow the conversation to wonder.
- Stay calm and let the customer know you'll take care of his problem.
- Don't use overly technical language with a customer. There is no need to impress the customer with your knowledge.
- Show respect for the customer, his choice of brands and products, and his property.
- Speak in complete sentences.
- Your company's policy about customer interaction is called a Service Level Agreement.

Allow the customer to complete statements – avoid interrupting

- Don't interrupt the customer. However, you can refuse to allow the conversation to get off base.

Clarify customer statements – ask pertinent questions

- Find out what happened just before the problem started, what has recently changed, how to reproduce the problem, and ask about any data that is not backed up.

Avoid using jargon, abbreviations, and acronyms

- Gauge the level of technical language you can use with the customer. Some customers are technically savvy; with these customers, it's okay to use technical language. For less experienced customers, be careful to not talk down to the customer or use terms he cannot understand.

Listen to customers

- Learn to be an active listener. Take notes; pause before speaking. If necessary, allow the customer to vent.
- A problem is not resolved until both you and the customer agree it is.
- If a coworker is having a problem dealing with a difficult customer, step in and offer to help.

- Be sure to complete all required paperwork for each troubleshooting situation. Record the initial symptoms, what you did to solve the problem, the underlying problem, and the resolution. When you first start troubleshooting, be sure to record information about the customer, hardware, software, and pertinent warranties.

USE JOB-RELATED PROFESSIONAL BEHAVIOR INCLUDING NOTATION OF PRIVACY, CONFIDENTIALITY, AND RESPECT FOR THE CUSTOMER AND CUSTOMERS' PROPERTY

Behavior

- *Maintain a positive attitude and tone of voice*
  - Customers expect a PC technician to remain professional at all times. Stay positive about the problem, your company, its products, and the customer.
- *Avoid arguing with customers and/or becoming defensive*
  - You are not required to defend your company or its products. If the customer has a complaint, take the information down or direct the customer to the appropriate person.
- *Do not minimize customers' problems*
  - Demonstrate to the customer that her problem is important to you.
  - Do not talk about other customer's problems as being more significant than the one at hand.
- *Avoid being judgmental and/or insulting or calling the customer names*
  - Stay professional at all times. Control your anger or frustration. Never complain or speak negatively about your company or products or your competitor's products.
  - Don't disparage the customer's choice of hardware or software. Allow the customer to vent when angry at you, your company, or your products. However, you are not required to endure abusive language.
- *Avoid distractions and/or interruptions when talking with customers*
  - Do not make or answer personal calls while working with a customer or at the customer site.
  - Know and follow your company's policy about answering your cell phone while working with the customer. Your company might require that you answer incoming calls from your company, even when you are speaking with a customer.

Property

- *Telephone, laptop, desktop computer, printer, monitor, etc.*
  - Respect the customer's property and privacy. Don't touch the customer's keyboard or mouse until given permission.
  - Do not open data files unless this is required to solve the problem. Protect any sensitive information on the desk or in the computer.
  - If you must call your company during an onsite visit and don't have a cell phone, ask permission before using the customer's telephone. Ask before printing to the printer.

SCENARIO 8.1: PRACTICE HELP DESK SKILLS

OBJECTIVES

The goal of this lab is to help you learn how to work with a customer using a chat session. After completing this lab, you will be able to:

- Use help desk skills in a chat session and on the phone to solve customer problems.

MATERIALS REQUIRED

This lab requires the following:

- Two or more Windows XP computers connected by the Internet or a network for each student workgroup
- Phone (cell phone works fine) for each student

LAB PREPARATION

Before the lab begins, the instructor or lab assistant needs to do the following:

- Make available two networked Windows XP computers for each student workgroup of two or more students.
- Tell students to bring their cell phone to lab or provide telephones in lab.

SCENARIO BACKGROUND

In the past, help desk support was solely by telephone, but more and more companies are offering technical support for their hardware and software products by way of chat sessions between the company help desk and the customer. Help desk personnel need to know how to ask questions, connect with the customer in a friendly and personal tone, and solve the customer's problem using telephone or chat. These chat sessions are typically started by clicking a link on the company's Web site. For example, in Figure 8-1, you can see where to click to start a live chat session with Linksys support.

SCENARIO

Jesse is having problems securing his wireless network. The multifunctional router that serves as his wireless access point was giving problems, so he pressed the Reset button on the router to give it a fresh start. The router began working, but he then discovered he had reset the router back to factory default settings, undoing all his wireless security settings. When Jesse tried to reconfigure the router, he could not find the router documentation, which included the username and password to the router firmware utility. After giving up his search for the documentation, he now decides to contact Linksys for help.

TROUBLESHOOTING

Jesse goes to the Linksys Web site and clicks the SUPPORT link, which opens the page shown in Figure 8-1. He clicks the Live Chat link, and on the next page, enters his name, phone number, e-mail address, and product name. After he submits this information, a chat window opens similar to the one in Figure 8-2. Drew is working the help desk at Linksys and responds.

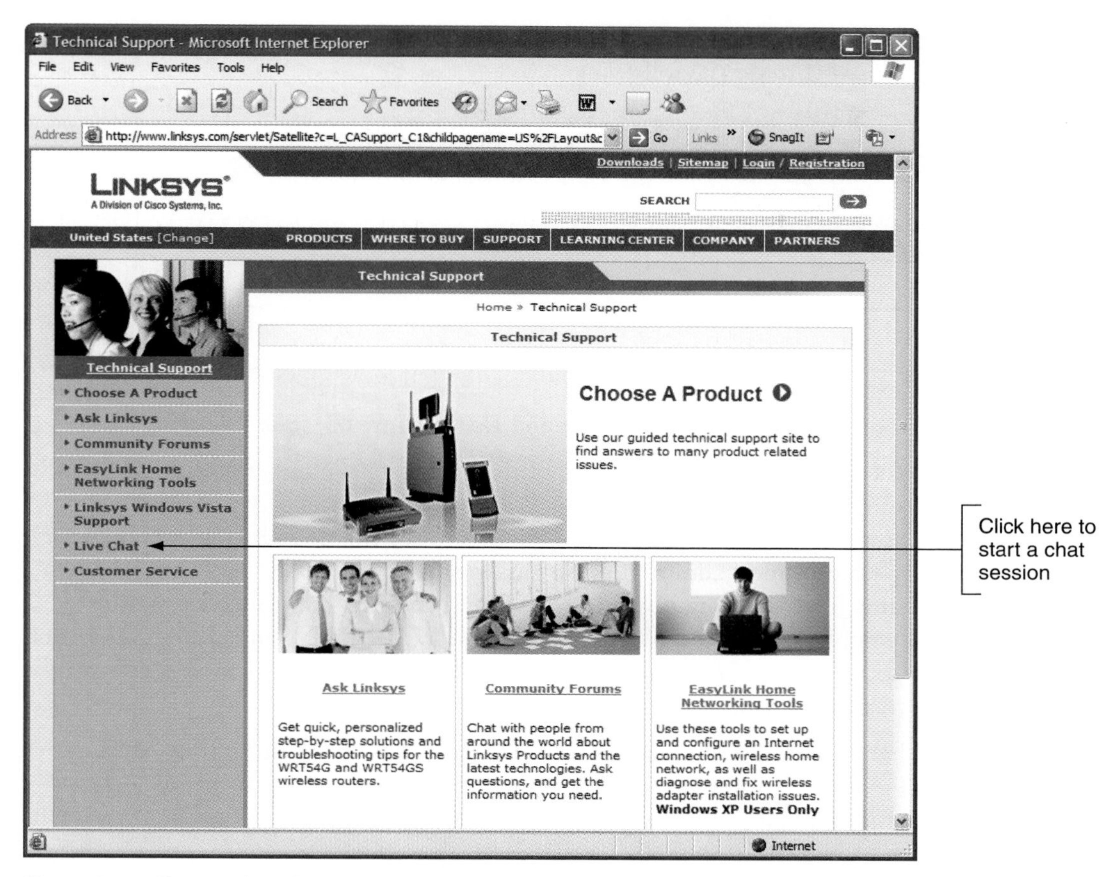

Figure 8-1 Chat sessions for technical support are often available by way of manufacturer Web sites

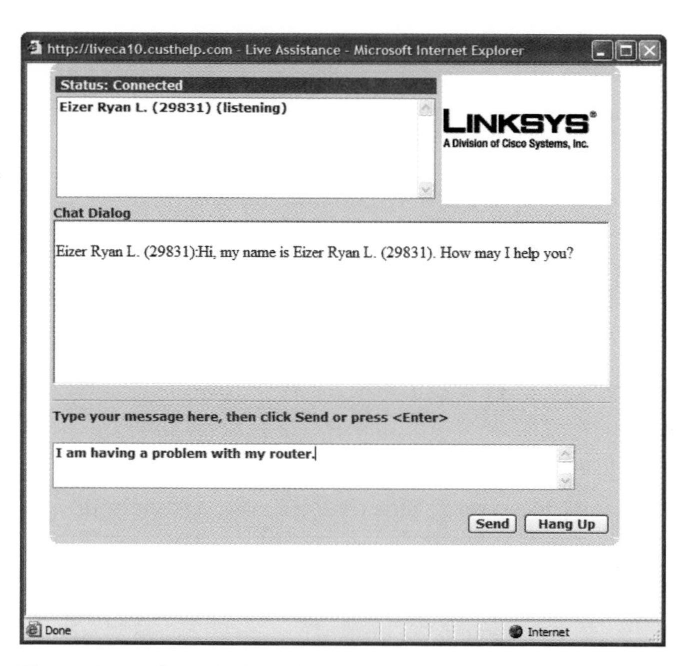

Figure 8-2 Chat window with technical support

Working with a partner in your workgroup, use your network and chat software such as MSN Messenger or AIM to do the following:

1. Select one person in your workgroup to play the role of Jesse, the customer. Select another person to play the role of Drew, the help desk technician.
2. Jesse initiates a chat session with Drew. What is the first thing Drew says to Jesse in the chat session?

____

____

3. Complete the chat session between Jesse and Drew. Drew does the following:
   - Drew asks Jesse for the serial number of the router. This number is embedded on the bottom of the router.
   - Drew knows the default username and password for this router to be a blank entry for the username and "admin" for the password.
   - Drew wants Jesse to know it would have been better for him to have reset the router by unplugging it and plugging it back in, rather than using the Reset button.
   - Drew also suggests to Jesse that for security reasons, he needs to enter a new username and password for the router.
4. Print the chat session. If your chat software does not have the print option, then copy and paste the chat session text into a document and print the document. As a courtesy to their customers, many companies e-mail to the customer a transcription of the chat session with technical support.
5. Critique the chat session with others in your workgroup. Make suggestions that might help Drew to be more effective, friendly, and helpful.

____

____

Use telephones to simulate a help desk conversation. Use the same troubleshooting scenario, but this time reverse roles between Jesse and Drew. Do the following:

1. Jesse calls Drew, and Drew answers, "Hello, this is Drew Jackson with the Linksys help desk. May I please have your name, the product you need help with, your phone number, and e-mail address."
2. After the information is collected, Drew allows Jesse to describe the problem and steps him through the solution.
3. When the problem is solved, Drew ends the call politely and positively.
4. Make suggestions that might help Drew to be more effective, friendly, and helpful.

____

____

In the next help desk sessions, Joy contacts technical support for her company complaining of too many pop-up ads on her desktop. Do the following:

1. Select someone to play the role of Joy and another to play the role of Sam, the help desk technician.
2. Using chat software, Joy starts a chat session with Sam, and Sam solves the problem. Assume that Joy is a novice user that needs a little extra help with keystrokes.
3. Sam decides to have Joy turn on the IE 6 pop-up blocker, use previously installed antivirus software to scan for viruses, and download, install, and run Windows Defender software from the Microsoft Web site.
4. Print the chat session and discuss it with the workgroup. Do you have any suggestions for Sam to improve his help desk skills?

   ____

   ____

   ____

5. Using telephones, reverse roles for Joy and Sam and solve the same problem. Do you have any suggestions for Sam to improve his help desk skills?

   ____

   ____

   ____

REVIEW QUESTIONS

1. After doing your best but finding you still cannot solve a customer's problem, what is the appropriate next step?

   ____

2. Your cell phone rings while working with a customer. You look at the incoming number and realize it's your sister calling. How do you handle the call?

   ____

3. Why is it not a good idea to tell a customer about the time you were able to solve the computer problem of a very important person?

   ____

4. A customer is angry and tells you he will never buy another product from your company again. How do you respond?

   ____

SCENARIO 8.2: PRACTICE SKILLS FOR GOOD COMMUNICATION

OBJECTIVES

The goal of this lab is to help you learn how to be a better communicator. After completing this lab, you will be able to:

- Be a better listener.
- Work with a customer who is angry.
- Act with integrity to customers.

MATERIALS REQUIRED

This lab requires the following:

- Student workgroups of two or more students

LAB PREPARATION

No lab preparation is necessary.

SCENARIO BACKGROUND

PC support technicians are expected to be good communicators. Many times, technical people find this to be a difficult skill, so practice and training is very important. In this lab, you discover some ways to be an active listener and better communicator.

SCENARIO

Work with a partner to learn to be a better listener. Do the following:

1. Sit with paper and pencil before another student who will play the role of a customer. As the customer describes a certain computer problem he or she is having, take notes as necessary.
2. Describe the problem back to the customer. Were you able to describe the problem accurately without any missing details? Have the customer rate you from one to ten, ten being the highest rating for good listening skills.

   ____

3. Now switch roles as you, the customer, describe a problem to the support technician. Then have the technician repeat the problem and its details. Rate the technician for good listening skills on a scale of one to ten.

   ____

4. Now describe an increasingly more difficult problem with more details. Rate the technician on a scale of one to ten for good listening skills.

   ____

5. Switch roles and listen to a detailed, difficult problem described. Then repeat the problem and have the customer rate your listening skills.

____

Being a good communicator requires being able to deal with angry and difficult people. Make suggestions as to the best way to handle these situations:

1. An angry customer calls to tell you that she has left you numerous phone messages that you have not answered. She is not aware that you receive about 25 voice messages a day and are trying hard to keep up with the workload. What do you say?

____

____

2. What can you say when an angry customer begins to use abusive language?

____

____

3. You have tried for over two hours, but cannot fix the customer's boot problem. You think the motherboard has failed, but you are not sure. Before you make your conclusions, you want to try a POST diagnostic card. The customer demands that you fix the problem immediately before she leaves the office at 4:45pm—about ten minutes from now. What do you say to her?

____

____

4. Discuss your answers with others in your workgroup.

Discuss in your workgroup the ethical thing to do in each situation below. Write down the group consensus to each problem:

1. You work on commission in a computer retail store, and after working with a very difficult customer for over an hour, he leaves without buying a thing. As he walks out the door, you notice he dropped a twenty-dollar bill near where you were talking. What do you do?

____

____

2. A customer is yelling at a coworker in a retail store. You see your coworker does not know how to handle the situation. What do you do?

____

____

3. You are working in a corporate office as a technical support person trying to fix a scanner problem at an employee's workstation. You notice the employee has left

payroll database information displayed on the screen. You know this employee is not authorized to view this information. What do you do?

____

____

4. Your supervisor has asked you to install a game on his computer. The game is on a CD-R and is obviously a pirated copy. What do you do?

____

____

5. You work for a retail store that sells a particular brand of computers. A customer asks your opinion of another brand of computer. What do you do?

____

____

6. You are asked to make a house call to fix a computer problem. When you arrive at the appointed time, a teenage girl answers the door and tells you her mother is not at home, but will return in a half hour. What do you do?

____

____

Have a little fun with this one! Working in a group of three, one member of the team plays the role of tech support. A second team member writes down a brief description of a difficult customer and passes the description to a third team member. (The tech support person cannot see this description.) The third team member plays out the described customer role. Use the following scenarios:

1. A customer calls to say his notebook will not start. The LCD panel was broken when the customer dropped the notebook, but he does not willingly disclose the fact that the notebook was dropped.
2. A customer complains the CD drive does not work. The CD is in the drive upside down, but the customer does not want the tech to ask him such a simple question.

REVIEW QUESTIONS

1. When working at a retail store that also fixes computers, list five items of information you should take when a customer first brings a computer to your counter.

____

2. List three things you should not do while at a customer's site.

____

3. When is it acceptable to ask a customer to refrain from venting?

____

4. When is it appropriate to answer a cell phone call while working with a customer?

____

5. When is it appropriate to install pirated software on a computer?

____

PRACTICE EXAM

The following practice exam covers the domain, *Communication and Professionalism*.

1. A customer complains that the antivirus software you installed on her computer has allowed a virus to infect her system. When you check her computer, you discover she does not have the AV software set to automatically download virus definitions or scan incoming e-mail in the background. You know that you set the software to do these things when you installed it. How do you handle the problem?
   a. Run the AV software to clean her system and reconfigure it for automatic updating and scanning
   b. Sit with the customer and show her how to scan the system for viruses and configure the AV software for automatic updates and scanning
   c. Tell the customer that if she insists on making changes to the AV software you have installed, you will not be able to service her computer in the future
   d. Explain to the customer that she caused the problem by reconfiguring the software and then fix the problem
2. An internal customer calls you to his workstation to help him install Microsoft Office from CD. After the installation is complete, he asks you to install one more program: a game that he has burned on a CD-R. What do you do?
   a. Do not install the game and tell your manager about the customer's request
   b. Do not install the game and suggest to the customer's manager that he should instruct his employees about software piracy
   c. Tell the customer you cannot install unauthorized software on company computers
   d. Install the game and ask to borrow the CD-R for your own computer
3. You are working at a help desk and an angry customer calls you and curses as he explains his problem. What do you do?
   a. Solve his problem and then tell your manager about this customer
   b. Tell the customer he must calm down and stop cursing before you can solve his problem
   c. Shout at the customer and let him know you will match his language if necessary
   d. Hang up on the customer
4. You work in a computer retail store, and a customer who is considering a purchase complains that your product is inferior to another brand. You are certain this is not

true, and, in fact, know the other product has numerous problems and faults. How do you handle the conversation?

a. Tell the customer about the problems and faults of the other brand

b. Explain to the customer the benefits of your product, but do not disparage the competing product

c. Ask the customer if he would like to *really* know about this other product. If he says yes, then tell him all you know

d. Tell the customer if he feels that strongly about the other product, he should just go buy it

5. Linda works at a local computer store and arrives at a home in response to a request for a house call. The owner answers the door and shows her to the computer. While Linda is working on the computer, the woman comes to tell her that she is stepping out for a few minutes and, if Linda needs anything, to ask her 10-year-old son who is watching TV in his room. What does Linda do?

   a. Tell the owner she cannot be alone in the house with a minor

   b. Finish fixing the computer problem and wait for the owner to return home to check her work

   c. Ask the owner for her cell phone number in case there is a problem

   d. Call her manager to ask him what she should do

6. You are working on a computer problem in the presence of the customer and your cell phone rings. You look at the incoming number and recognize it is your biggest customer. What do you do?

   a. Excuse yourself from the room and answer the phone

   b. Answer the phone in the presence of the customer

   c. Allow the call to forward to voice mail

   d. Don't answer the call, but tell the customer you have to go to your car to research his problem. When you get to your car, return the call.

7. You are working at a customer site and the work is taking longer than expected. You are expected at a meeting with your supervisor and recognize that you are not going to finish the work in time to make the meeting. What do you do?

   a. Finish the work and later explain to your supervisor what happened

   b. Tell the customer you have an important meeting and will return later that day to finish the work

   c. Tell the customer you are not feeling well and need to leave

   d. Call your supervisor and ask him what he wants you to do

8. You have done your very best to fix a customer's problem, but you don't know what else to try. What do you do next?

   a. Escalate the problem to the next level of support in your organization

   b. Ask a coworker for ideas or suggestions

c. Tell the customer you are very sorry but you cannot fix his problem

d. Tell the customer his computer cannot be fixed and needs replacing

9. A customer brings in a printer to your shop, tells you it is defective, and asks for a replacement at no cost. You look at the printer and suspect it has been dropped. What do you do?

   a. Say to the customer, "We will not replace this printer because you have dropped it"

   b. Ask the customer, "Is it possible the printer was dropped?"

   c. Say to the customer, "This printer is not defective"

   d. Tell the customer you think she is lying

10. You arrive at an employee's workstation to help her solve her computer problem. She tells you her CD drive is broken and asks you to replace it. What do you do next?

    a. Ask her to show you the problem she is having with the drive

    b. Shut down the computer and check the internal cables to the drive to make sure the connections are solid

    c. Ask her why she thinks the drive is broken

    d. Check Device Manager to see if Windows reports errors about the drive

    e. Tell her you will return as soon as you find a new drive

11. When solving a problem on the phone with a customer, which best describes how to handle off-the-subject conversation?

    a. Stay on the subject and don't talk about anything except the problem at hand

    b. Show the customer you are friendly by asking about his/her personal life

    c. Include a little friendly chitchat but don't overdo it

    d. Tell the customer about other customers and their problems to make the customer feel they are not alone in their problems

12. Mr. Jones, a customer, has made you very angry by his negative accusations against you and your work. You feel you have done a good job to serve him, and the problem is his attitude. What do you do?

    a. Call Mr. Jones and explain to him that you have done your best to serve him

    b. Tell your coworkers about what Mr. Jones said and ask if any of them have ever had to deal with Mr. Jones. Find out how they handled him.

    c. Describe the problem to a coworker, but don't use the customer's name. Ask the coworker for suggestions as to how to handle the problem.

    d. Wait until you get home and complain to your family about Mr. Jones and his problems

13. A customer calls to say her CD drive does not work. You ask her to open the drive and verify the CD is right side up. She tells you it is. When you arrive at her desk, you discover the CD is face down. What do you do?

    a. Flip the CD over and verify the drive is working

    b. Say to her, "I told you to check if the CD is right side up"

c. Tell her she needs to learn more about how CDs work

d. Flip the CD over and return to your desk

14. You work at a computer retail store and overhear a coworker having a difficult time with an unhappy customer. What do you do?

a. Tell your manager about the problem

b. Do nothing. Your coworker will ask for help if he needs it.

c. Walk over and ask your coworker if you can help

d. Tell the customer that your coworker is having a hard day and offer to help the customer

15. A customer asks you to fix his printing problem. While you are working on the problem, he leaves you and the computer to take a break. When he returns, the problem is fixed, but you have had to wait for 10 minutes so that he can sign the technical support ticket. What do you do?

a. Ask him to sign the ticket and leave

b. Ask him to verify that he can print

c. Explain to the customer that you have waited 10 minutes after you fixed the problem

d. Tell the customer he has just wasted your time

Acronyms

CompTIA provides a list of acronyms you need to know before you take the A+ exams. You can download the list from the CompTIA Web site at *www.comptia.org*. The list is included here for your convenience. However, CompTIA occasionally updates the list, so be sure to check the CompTIA Web site for the latest version.

Acronym	Spelled Out
AC	alternating current
ACPI	advanced configuration and power interface
ACT	activity
ADSL	asymmetrical digital subscriber line
AGP	accelerated graphics port
AMD	advanced micro devices
AMR	audio modem riser
APIPA	automatic private Internet protocol addressing
APM	advanced power management
ARP	address resolution protocol
ASR	automated system recovery
AT	advanced technology
ATA	advanced technology attachment
ATAPI	advanced technology attachment packet interface
ATM	asynchronous transfer mode
ATX	advanced technology extended
BIOS	basic input/output system
BNC	Bayonet-Neill-Concelman or British Navel Connector
BRI	basic rate interface
BTX	balanced technology extended
CCD	charged coupled device
CD	compact disc
CD-ROM	compact disc-read-only memory
CD-RW	compact disc-rewritable
CDFS	compact disc file system
CMOS	complementary metal-oxide semiconductor
CNR	communication network riser
COM1	communication port 1
CPU	central processing unit
CRIMM	continuity-Rambus inline memory module
CRT	cathode-ray tube
DAC	discretionary access control
DB-25	serial communications D-shell connector, 25 pins
DB-9	9 pin D shell connector
DC	direct current
DDOS	distributed denial of service
DDR	double data-rate
DDR RAM	double data-rate random access memory
DDR SDRAM	double data-rate synchronous dynamic random access memory

Acronym	Spelled Out
DFS	distributed file system
DHCP	dynamic host configuration protocol
DIMM	dual inline memory module
DIN	Deutsche Industrie Norm
DIP	dual inline package
DLT	digital linear tape
DLP	digital light processing
DMA	direct memory access
DNS	domain name service or domain name server
DOS	disk operating system or denial of service
DPMS	display power management signaling
DRAM	dynamic random access memory
DSL	digital subscriber line
DVD	digital video disc or digital versatile disc
DVD-RAM	digital video disc-random access memory
DVD-ROM	digital video disc-read-only memory
DVD-R	digital video disc-recordable
DVD-RW	digital video disc-rewritable
DVI	digital visual interface
ECC	error correction code
ECP	extended capabilities port
EEPROM	electrically erasable programmable read-only memory
EFS	encrypting file system
EIDE	enhanced integrated drive electronics
EISA	extended industry standard architecture
EMI	electromagnetic interference
EMP	electromagnetic pulse
EPROM	erasable programmable read-only memory
EPP	enhanced parallel port
ERD	emergency repair disk
ESD	electrostatic discharge
ESDI	enhanced small device interface
EVGA	extended video graphics adapter/array
EVDO	evolution data optimized or evolution data only
FAT	file allocation table
FAT12	12-bit file allocation table
FAT16	16-bit file allocation table
FAT32	32-bit file allocation table
FDD	floppy disk drive

Acronym	Spelled Out
FERPA	Family Educational Rights and Privacy Act
Fn	Function (referring to the function key on a laptop)
FPM	fast page-mode
FRU	field replaceable unit
FTP	file transfer protocol
FQDN	fully qualified domain name
GB	gigabyte
GDI	graphics device interface
GHz	gigahertz
GUI	graphical user interface
GPRS	general packet radio system
GSM	global system for mobile communications
HAL	hardware abstraction layer
HCL	hardware compatibility list
HDD	hard disk drive
HDMi	high definition media interface
HPFS	high performance file system
HTML	hypertext markup language
HTTP	hypertext transfer protocol
HTTPS	hypertext transfer protocol over secure sockets layer
I/O	input/output
ICMP	Internet control message protocol
ICS	Internet connection sharing
ICR	intelligent character recognition
IDE	integrated drive electronics
IEEE	Institute of Electrical and Electronics Engineers
IIS	Internet Information Services
IMAP	Internet mail access protocol
IP	Internet protocol
IPCONFIG	Internet protocol configuration
IPP	Internet printing protocol
IPSEC	Internet protocol security
IPX	internetwork packet exchange
IPX/SPX	internetwork packet exchange/sequenced packet exchange
IR	infrared
IrDA	Infrared Data Association
IRQ	interrupt request
ISA	industry standard architecture
ISDN	integrated services digital network

Acronym	Spelled Out
ISO	Industry Standards Organization
ISP	Internet service provider
KB	kilobyte
LAN	local area network
LBA	logical block addressing
LC	Lucent connector
LCD	liquid crystal display
LDAP	lightweight directory access protocol
LED	light emitting diode
LIP or LiPoly	lithium-ion polymer Li-on lithium-ion
LPD/LPR	line printer daemon/line printer remote
LPT	line printer terminal
LPT1	line printer terminal 1
LPX	low profile extended
LVD	low voltage differential
MAC	media access control
MAN	metropolitan area network
MAPI	messaging application programming interface
Mb	megabit
MB	megabyte
MBR	master boot record
MBSA	Microsoft Baseline Security Analyzer
MCR	multivariant curve resolution
MFD	multi-function device
MFP	multi-function product
MHz	megahertz
MicroDIMM	micro dual inline memory module
MIDI	musical instrument digital interface
MIME	multipurpose Internet mail extension
MLI	multiple link interface
MMC	Microsoft management console
MMX	multimedia extensions
MP3	Moving Picture Experts Group Layer 3 Audio
MPEG	Moving Picture Experts Group
MSCONFIG	Microsoft configuration
MSDS	material safety data sheet
MUI	multilingual user interface
NAS	network-attached storage
NAT	network address translation

Acronym	Spelled Out
NetBIOS	networked basic input/output system
NetBEUI	networked basic input/output system extended user interface
NFS	network file system
NIC	network interface card
NiCd	nickel cadmium
NiMH	nickel metal hydride
NLI	not logged in or natural language interface
NLX	new low-profile extended
NNTP	network news transfer protocol
NTFS	new technology file system
NTLDR	new technology loader
NWLINK	Netware Link
OCR	optical character recognition
OEM	original equipment manufacturer
OMR	optical mark recognition
OS	operating system
OSR	original equipment manufacturer service release
PAN	personal area network
PATA	parallel advanced technology attachment
PC	personal computer
PCI	peripheral component interconnect
PCIe	peripheral component interconnect express
PCIX	peripheral component interconnect extended
PCL	printer control language
PCMCIA	Personal Computer Memory Card International Association
PDA	personal digital assistant
PGA	pin grid array
PGA2	pin grid array 2
PIN	personal identification number
PKI	public key infrastructure
PnP	plug and play
POP	post office protocol
POP3	post office protocol 3
POST	power-on self test
POTS	plain old telephone service
PPP	point-to-point protocol
PPTP	point-to-point tunneling protocol
PRI	primary rate interface
PROM	programmable read-only memory

Acronym	Spelled Out
PS/2	Personal System/2 connector
PSTN	public switched telephone network
PVCPXE	permanent virtual circuit preboot execution environment
QoS	quality of service
RAID	redundant array of independent (or inexpensive) discs
RAM	random access memory
RAS	remote access service
RBAC	role-based access control or rule-based access control
RDRAM	RAMBUS dynamic random access memory
RFRFI	radio frequency radio frequency interference
RGB	red green blue
RIMM	RAMBUS inline memory module
RIP	routing information protocol
RIS	remote installation service
RISC	reduced instruction set computer
RJ	registered jack
RJ-11	registered jack function 11
RJ-45	registered jack function 45
RMA	returned materials authorization
ROM	read-only memory
RS-232 or RS-232C	recommended standard 232
RTC	real-time clock
SAN	storage area network
SATA	serial advanced technology attachment
SC	subscription channel
SCSI	small computer system interface
SCSI ID	small computer system interface identifier
SD card	secure digital card
SDRAM	synchronous dynamic random access memory
SEC	single edge connector
SFC	system file checker
SGRAM	synchronous graphics random access memory
SIMM	single inline memory module
SLI	scalable link interface or system level integration or scanline interleave mode
SMB	server message block or small to midsize business
SMTP	simple mail transport protocol
SNMP	simple network management protocol
SoDIMM	small outline dual inline memory module
SOHO	small office/home office

Acronym	Spelled Out
SP	service pack
SP1	service pack 1
SP2	service pack 2
SPDIF	Sony-Philips digital interface format
SPGA	staggered pin grid array
SPX	sequenced package exchange
SRAM	static random access memory
SSH	secure shell
SSID	service set identifier
SSL	secure sockets layer
ST	straight tip
STP	shielded twisted pair
SVGA	super video graphics array
SXGA	super extended graphics array
TB	terabyte
TCP	transmission control protocol
TCP/IP	transmission control protocol/Internet protocol
TDR	time domain reflectometer
TFTP	trivial file transfer protocol
UART	universal asynchronous receiver transmitter
UDF	user defined functions or universal disk format or universal data format
UDMA	ultra direct memory access
UDP	user datagram protocol
UL	Underwriter's Laboratory
UNC	universal naming convention
UPS	uninterruptible power supply
URL	uniform resource locator
USB	universal serial bus
USMT	user state migration tool
UTP	unshielded twisted pair
UXGA	ultra extended graphics array
VESA	Video Electronics Standards Association
VFAT	virtual file allocation table
VGA	video graphics array
VoIP	voice over Internet protocol
VPN	virtual private network
VRAM	video random access memory
WAN	wide area network
WAP	wireless application protocol

Acronym	Spelled Out
WEP	wired equivalent privacy
WIFI	wireless fidelity
WINS	windows Internet name service
WLAN	wireless local area network
WPA	wireless protected access
WUXGA	wide ultra extended graphics array
XGA	extended graphics array
ZIF	zero-insertion-force
ZIP	zigzag inline package

APPENDIX B

Practice Exam Answers

This appendix contains the answers to the odd-numbered questions in the Practice Exams at the end of each chapter.

PRACTICE EXAM: CHAPTER 1

Correct answers for the Chapter 1 Practice Exam, odd-numbered questions only:

1. **c.** 240-pin DIMMs
3. **a.** If the hard drive has a PATA connector, you can use a PATA-to-SATA adapter to connect it to the SATA interface
5. **c.** Clean the mouse rollers using a cotton swab and a small amount of liquid soap
7. **b.** 133 MB/sec
9. **b.** RAID 1
11. **b.** Use an optical drive cleaning kit to clean the drive
13. **d.** The jumpers on the two drives are not set correctly
15. **c.** Open the case and check the power connector to the motherboard

PRACTICE EXAM: CHAPTER 2

Correct answers for the Chapter 2 Practice Exam, odd-numbered questions only:

1. **a.** Change the brightness of the LCD panel

   c. Put the system into hibernation
3. **b.** Bluetooth
5. **b.** Cellular WAN PC Card

   c. 802.11g
7. **b.** Verify that the wireless switch near the hinge of her laptop is turned on

   c. Verify the LCD panel of her laptop is fully raised
9. **b.** Everything in RAM has been copied to the hard drive and the system is shut down
11. **c.** 802.11g
13. **b.** Use the Settings tab of the Display Properties window to extend the Windows desktop to the second monitor
15. **a.** You can install one Type I card and one Type II card in the single Type III slot

PRACTICE EXAM: CHAPTER 3

Correct answers for the Chapter 3 Practice Exam, odd-numbered questions only:

1. **a.** Start up the Windows desktop in Safe Mode and then copy the data to another media
3. **b.** When the Windows System Root folder is corrupted or missing
5. **b.** Press Ctrl+C

   d. Press Ctrl+Break

7. **c.** Ipconfig/All
9. **d.** Event Viewer
11. **c.** Folder Options
13. **b.** Converting the file system from NTFS to FAT32
15. **c.** Either answer a or b will work

PRACTICE EXAM: CHAPTER 4

Correct answers for the Chapter 4 Practice Exam, odd-numbered questions only:

1. **b.** The inside of the printer is dirty
   d. The guide rollers inside the paper trays are not aligned
   e. The paper is damp or the room is too humid
   f. A paper tray is overloaded with paper
3. **b.** Recalibrating the position of the print head
5. **c.** On the Configure tab of the printer Properties window, check Duplexing Unit
7. **c.** The printer needs calibrating using software from the printer manufacturer
   d. The ink cartridges need replacing
9. **b.** TWAIN
11. **c.** PNG
13. **b.** On John's computer, share the printer so that others on the network can access it as a network printer
15. **c.** The problem is not the printer itself

PRACTICE EXAM: CHAPTER 5

Correct answers for the Chapter 5 Practice Exam, odd-numbered questions only:

1. **c.** Install the network cable in a conduit and route the conduit through the walls and ceiling
3. **b.** 254.255.0.0
5. **b.** \\Gorilla\Research
7. **c.** The computer cannot connect to the network
9. **d.** The ISP uses dynamic IP addressing
11. **c.** Nslookup
13. **b.** Configure TCP/IP for dynamic IP addressing and, on the Alternate Configuration tab, configure the settings for static IP addressing
15. **a.** Ping 127.0.0.1

PRACTICE EXAM: CHAPTER 6

Correct answers for the Chapter 6 Practice Exam, odd-numbered questions only:

1. **b.** Log in as an administrator
3. **c.** Mary can only read, but cannot edit or delete files in the folder
5. **d.** Log the employee off her workstation
7. **b.** Turn off simple file sharing and set permission for the folder so that only authorized users can view and modify the folder

   c. Use better security for the wireless network including MAC address filtering and data encryption
9. **a.** Require a six-character password and a smart card scan
11. **b.** WPA encryption
13. **a.** Verify the company uses static IP addressing for Internet access and configure the router for port forwarding
15. **b.** Update the AV software with the latest virus definitions

PRACTICE EXAM: CHAPTER 7

Correct answers for the Chapter 7 Practice Exam, odd-numbered questions only:

1. **b.** Isopropyl alcohol
3. **d.** To eliminate static electricity between you and the case
5. **d.** Check that the mouse is not sitting on glass or a similar shiny surface
7. **a.** Because plastic is not a good conductor
9. **a.** Work inside a power supply
11. **a.** Network card
13. **d.** Recommend to the customer he move the case to a safer location.
15. **d.** Shut down the computer

PRACTICE EXAM: CHAPTER 8

Correct answers for the Chapter 8 Practice Exam, odd-numbered questions only:

1. **b.** Sit with the customer and show her how to scan the system for viruses and configure the AV software for automatic updates and scanning
3. **b.** Tell the customer he must calm down and stop cursing before you can solve his problem
5. **a.** Tell the owner she cannot be alone in the house with a minor
7. **d.** Call your supervisor and ask him what he wants you to do

9. **b.** Ask the customer, “Is it possible the printer was dropped?”
11. **c.** Include a little friendly chitchat but don’t overdo it
13. **a.** Flip the CD over and verify the drive is working
15. **b.** Ask him to verify that he can print

INDEX